Mindfulness Therapy

How to Create Zen Peace, Happiness and Success
in Your Life

(The Best Guides for Practicing Buddhism,
Chakras and Mindfulness Meditation)

Michael Rowe

Published by Rob Miles

© **Michael Rowe**

All Rights Reserved

Mindfulness Therapy: How to Create Zen Peace, Happiness and Success in Your Life (The Best Guides for Practicing Buddhism, Chakras and Mindfulness Meditation)

ISBN 978-1-990084-12-6

All rights reserved. No part of this guide may be reproduced in any form without permission in writing from the publisher except in the case of brief quotations embodied in critical articles or reviews.

Legal & Disclaimer

The information contained in this book is not designed to replace or take the place of any form of medicine or professional medical advice. The information in this book has been provided for educational and entertainment purposes only.

The information contained in this book has been compiled from sources deemed reliable, and it is accurate to the best of the Author's knowledge; however, the Author cannot guarantee its accuracy and validity and cannot be held liable for any errors or omissions. Changes are periodically made to this book. You must consult your doctor or get professional medical advice before using any of the suggested remedies, techniques, or information in this book.

Upon using the information contained in this book, you agree to hold harmless the Author from and against any damages, costs, and expenses, including any legal fees potentially resulting from the application of any of the information provided by this guide. This disclaimer applies to any damages or injury caused by the use and application, whether directly or indirectly, of any advice or information presented, whether for breach of contract, tort, negligence, personal injury, criminal intent, or under any other cause of action.

You agree to accept all risks of using the information presented inside this book. You need to consult a professional medical practitioner in order to ensure you are both able and healthy enough to participate in this program.

Table of Contents

INTRODUCTION 1

CHAPTER 1: UNDERSTANDING THE NEED FOR MINDFULNESS 5

CHAPTER 2: THE PURPOSE OF MINDFULNESS 13

CHAPTER 3: MINDFUL MEDITATION EXPLAINED 22

CHAPTER 4: WHO DO YOU THINK YOU ARE? 27

CHAPTER 5: THE SCHOOL OF ZEN 33

CHAPTER 6: THE POWER OF NEUROTRANSMITTERS 37

CHAPTER 7: MINDFULNESS-BASED STRESS REDUCTION AND MINDFULNESS EXERCISES 47

CHAPTER 8: TECHNIQUES TO DEVELOP THE MINDFUL KID 69

CHAPTER 9: CREATING HEALTHY RELATIONSHIPS 92

CHAPTER 10: BEGINNING MINDFUL MEDITATION 99

CHAPTER 11: HOW MEDITATIVE PRACTICES "REWIRE" YOUR BRAIN 105

CHAPTER 12: BENEFITS OF MINDFULNESS MEDITATION 122

CHAPTER 13: WHAT IS MINDFULNESS AND HOW IT FUELS PRODUCTIVITY? 131

CHAPTER 14: IMPORTANCE OF BOUNDARIES 139

CHAPTER 15: EXPERIMENT WITH THE DIFFERENT FORMS OF MINDFULNESS 146

CHAPTER 16: CREATING HEALTHY RELATIONSHIPS 155

CHAPTER 17: HOW TO PRACTICE MEDITATION 162

CHAPTER 18: HEALTH BENEFITS OF MINDFULNESS 181

CHAPTER 19: OTHER ALTERNATIVE WAYS TO DEAL WITH ANXIETY 186

CONCLUSION 198

Introduction

It's not just about reducing stress or letting go and taking a few moments for ourselves to try and recompose and regain our thoughts. Meditation is about more than that.

It is about finding balance, inner peace, and calm in a world where it seems almost every aspect of our lives is capable of triggering stress, worry, or anxiety. Our bodies and minds may be strong and tough, but there is only so much negativity that it can take before it starts to take its toll and affect our health, sometimes to a point where it could become unbearable. If only there were a magic formula of some sort where we could keep out these negative feelings that are capable of causing such destruction within our minds and bodies, but there isn't. Which is why, we need to turn to meditation as a way of managing our worries and anxieties, to find a way to find that balance within ourselves and recharge our energy.

The beauty of meditation is that it is simple yet powerful. Simple enough that anyone can learn how to do it effectively with the right tools, teachings, and techniques. Anyone can learn the art of meditation, and it isn't as difficult as you may imagine. Sure, you may have tried it a few times and found yourself struggling in the early stages to quiet your mind and achieve a focus, calm, and mindful state, but that is perfectly normal, especially if you're a beginner just starting out on this journey.

The following chapters will discuss everything you need to begin a meditation practice—from the correct posture to use to various techniques to employ for the most successful experience. Along the way, different ideas will be discussed and will explore the nature of meditation, including the difference in perspective between practical and spiritual meditation. There are many reasons to meditate—from proven health benefits to greater success in life to achieving mental states through dedication to the practice. The emphasis in this book will be on achieving happiness through a practical, step-by-step approach to techniques developed over thousands of years. Along the way, you will read about options you can choose to take your meditation to the next level, engaging in an ancient wisdom to achieve the ultimate goal of all meditation—enlightenment.

Mastering the art of meditation, like everything else, takes patience, time and practice. You're putting far too much pressure on yourself if you expect to get it right from the moment you sit cross-legged on your mat and shut your eyes hoping to achieve deep meditation right from the get-go. No, it takes time and practice, and you need to be patient with yourself. Practice makes perfect, which is why your goal of achieving deep meditation is spread out over four weeks. You need time to master each stage and phase of the process before moving onto the next. With repeated effort and your goal clearly in mind, you will see results at the end of the four weeks.

Chapter 1: Understanding The Need For Mindfulness

It is impossible to master any art without gaining full knowledge of what it is. To start being mindful, therefore, you need to learn more about mindfulness.

Life happens every moment; unfortunately, we miss the best part of the whole show. If you know next to nothing about mindfulness or how you can live a mindful life, it is easy to let the present moment slip away unobserved. When you spend your time worrying about the opportunities you missed or lost in the past or what the future holds, you squander life's most precious moments: the present moment.

In today's busy world, it is easy to ruminate on a not-so-beautiful past or worry about a not-so-guaranteed future. Trust today's world to supply you with more than enough reasons to keep you distracted, fragmented, and disintegrated without any time to engage in practices that can help you enjoy calmness and stillness.

At work, you hardly concentrate on the present tasks. Instead, you think and fantasize over the dream vacation to Honolulu Island. When you finally manage to save up money and find the time to go for that vacation you have been dreaming about for years, you find your mind drifting to the tasks on your desk waiting for you to be done with the vacation and return to give them the attention they deserve.

Mindfulness is your best route of escape from this never-ending cycle of intrusive memories from your ugly past and fretful feelings about what may or may not happen in the future. Mindfulness saves you from what Buddhists refer to as the monkey-mind, a phrase used to describe a mind that tends to jump from one irrelevant thought to another just like monkeys hop from one tree branch to another.

When you master the art of mindful living as contained in the pages of this guide, you will gain the ability to observe your thoughts with full awareness instead of allowing these thoughts to control you.

Mindfulness Defined

Wikipedia, defines mindfulness as the psychological process of bringing your attention to experiences occurring in the present moment. It goes on to say you can develop mindfulness through the process of meditation and several other mindful training techniques.

Basic Points to Note about Mindfulness

Mindfulness is not a spiritual exercise: Some people attribute mindfulness to certain spiritual connections. While the origin of this technique traces back to Indian Hindu practices, it has gone beyond what it used to be when in its infancy. Today, mindfulness is a holistic practice anyone can practice irrespective of religion, tribe, or skin color and still get the same results.

There is nothing harmful about mindful techniques: Engaging in mindful meditation and other mindful techniques does not harm you in any way or establish any kind of spiritual link between you and any astral beings as some myths claim. Mindfulness concentrates on things you do daily; it only teaches you to do them with increased concentration.

Benefits of Mindfulness

There are several ways mindful living improves your overall quality of life. Let us discuss some of the major benefits of living mindfully:

Self-discovery: Knowing your true self, your purpose for living, and innate abilities is possible only when you learn to live a more mindful life and pay more attention to areas you have ignored all your life. Sometimes we miss our life's purpose because we do not know where skills, passions, desires, and abilities tilt towards and what we should do with all the universe has given us as inborn talents. Mindfulness helps you discover the real you and what direction your life should be taking.

Increased concentration: One major thing mindful living helps you achieve is enhanced concentration and focus. As you engage in mindful techniques and exercises aimed at helping you calm your mind and nerves, you gain the ability to focus and concentrate more on things that matter the most in your life. The more mindful you become and enjoy life as it happens, the less you will worry about a future you cannot foretell and a past you cannot change.

Less anxiety, depression, and stress: When left unattended to for too long, the cascade of disturbing thoughts flowing in and out of your mind daily has a way of keeping you depressed, stressed out, and anxious. Mindfulness helps you live a life of gratitude and appreciate all the positive things you have working for you rather than dwell on the negatives and bad side of life and life's events.

Relative peace and calmness: Mindfulness brings into your life a unique feeling of peace and tranquility. When you become mindful, negativities and toxins accumulated through years of negative thinking and worries will naturally flow out of your life. With that comes a feeling of peace nothing else can bring.

Acceptance: Your journey to true happiness and fulfillment begins when you learn to accept who you are the way you are. Accepting the things you cannot change will help you change the things you can change, which in turn helps you live a more fulfilling life.

Improved heath: Anxiety and worry can cause many diseases and trigger several negative reactions within the body. These reactions lead to over secretion of stress hormones and brain chemicals that can leave you sick and down with ailments such as indigestion, insomnia, high blood pressure, etc.

Healthier relationships: Nothing kills a relationship faster than not being present during conversations, sex, and every moment that means the world to your spouse. With an increased level of mindfulness, you pay enough attention to your spouse's body language, facial expressions, and mood. Because of this, you know when things are not as they ought to be and when something is bothering your partner. Further, mindfulness helps you make the sex and romance in your relationship something to look forward to since it teaches you to pay more attention to the desires of your body and that of your partner.

Now you know why you should work hard to make mindfulness an important part of your daily living.

Let us now look at how you can to start living a mindful life and start enjoying the peace and happiness it brings:

Chapter 2: The Purpose Of Mindfulness

We all experience change constantly. Consistently. Change is the main consistent nowadays. It occurs and it happens quick. What are you doing pretty much the majority of the adjustment in your life? It is safe to say that you are opposing it? Giving it a chance to wash by you? Grasping it? Giving it a chance to take you where it will? I envision that a large portion of us do these things dependent on the change that is occurring at the time. Be that as it may, what might it resemble on the off chance that we were more accountable for our reactions to change? What might it resemble on the off chance that we were increasingly out before it?

We can be on the off chance that we choose to lead a mindfulness and purposeful life. By driving a mindfulness and purposeful life I mean having an unmistakable mission, vision and set of qualities that guide our life and utilizing that to control by. When we utilize our own main goal, vision and qualities to manage us they act like a rudder giving us strength and helping us make course revisions as life gets extreme. They help us set our course when the going is smooth so as we see change seemingly within easy reach we have an approach to settle on choices about that change and can make sense of how to utilize it to further our potential benefit as opposed to consider it to be an immense hindrance.

Mindfulness and aim go past simply having an individual mission, vision and qualities. It is reflected by they way we approach our day by day living. It is reflected in the objectives we set for ourselves and by they way we approach achieving those objectives. Aim comes in with respect to how we address objective fulfillment. How are we going to approach accomplishing our objectives? How are we going to treat other individuals along the way? What is our goal with each activity that we choose to take. What is our goal with our responses to things? Deliberate individuals have a genuine reason set out about how they are going to appear on the planet and how they will associate with the individuals in it.

At last mindfulness becomes possibly the most important factor. A mindfulness individual is constantly mindful of himself and how he is collaborating with other individuals. He is completely mindful of how his activities sway others and of how they respond to him. He screens that and connects with his expectations to increase a beneficial outcome and result.

So you see goal and mindfulness have an inseparable tie to change - being responsible for the results of progress is a ground-breaking thing. Making sense of this isn't in every case simple. This may be an extraordinary time for you to get a mentor to help.

What is Mindfulness Meditation?

Mindfulness contemplation is a psychological preparing practice that includes concentrating your brain on your encounters (like your own feelings, musings, and sensations) right now.

Mindfulness reflection can include breathing practice, mental symbolism, familiarity with body and brain, and muscle and body unwinding.

One of the first institutionalized projects for mindfulness contemplation is the Mindfulness-Based Stress Reduction (MBSR) program, created by Jon Kabat-Zinn, PhD (who was an understudy of Buddhist priest and researcher Thich Nhat Hanh). MBSR centers around mindfulness and consideration regarding the present. Other streamlined, common mindfulness reflection mediations have been progressively joined into medicinal settings to treat pressure, torment, a sleeping disorder, and other wellbeing conditions.

Learning mindfulness intercession is direct, in any case, an instructor or program can help you as you start (especially in case you're doing it for wellbeing purposes). A few people do it for 10 minutes, yet even a couple of minutes consistently can have any kind of effect. Here is a fundamental method for you to begin:

1. Locate a peaceful and agreeable spot. Sit in a seat or on the floor with your head, neck, and back straight however not firm.

2. Attempt to set aside all memories and the future and remain in the present.

3. Become mindful of your breath, concentrating on the impression of air moving all through your body as you relax. Feel your stomach rise and fall, and the air enter your noses and leave your mouth. Focus on the manner in which every breath changes and is extraordinary.

4. Watch each idea travel every which way, regardless of whether it be a stress, dread, tension or expectation. At the point

when considerations come up in your brain, don't disregard or smother them however essentially note them, keep quiet and utilize your breathing as a grapple.

5. If you end up escaping in your musings, see where your mind headed out to, without judging, and basically come back to your relaxing. Keep in mind not to be no picnic for yourself if this occurs.

6. As the opportunity arrives to a nearby, sit for a moment or two, getting to be mindful of where you are. Get up slowly.

Different Ways to Incorporate Mindfulness Into Your Life:

There's no law that says you should sit on a pad in a tranquil space to rehearse mindfulness, says Kate Hanley, creator of A Year of Daily Calm. Mindfulness intercession is one procedure, yet every day life gives a lot of chances to practice.3

Here are Kate Hanley's tips on developing mindfulness in your day by day schedule:

Doing the dishes. Have you at any point seen how nobody is attempting to stand out enough to be noticed while you're doing the dishes? The blend of alone time and physical action causes tidying to up after supper an incredible time to attempt a little mindfulness.

Brushing your teeth. You can't go a day without brushing your teeth, making this every day task the ideal chance to rehearse mindfulness. Feel your feet on the floor, the brush in your grasp, your arm going here and there. Einstein said he did his best reasoning while he was shaving- - I'd contend that what he was truly doing in those minutes was rehearsing mindfulness!

Driving. It's anything but difficult to daydream while you're driving, considering what to have for supper or what you neglected to do at work that day. Utilize your forces of mindfulness to keep your consideration moored to within your vehicle.

Mood killer the radio (or go it to something mitigating, similar to old style), envision your spine developing tall, locate the midpoint between loosening up your hands and holding the wheel too firmly, and take your consideration back to where you and your vehicle are in space at whatever point you see your mind meandering.

Working out. Truly, sitting in front of the TV while running on the treadmill will cause your exercise to go all the more rapidly, however it won't do a lot to calm your brain. Make your wellness attempts an activity in mindfulness by killing all screens and concentrating on your breathing and where your feet are in space as you move.

Sleep time. Watch your fights over sleep time with the children vanish when you quit attempting to hurry through it and basically attempt to appreciate the experience. Get down to a similar level as your children, look in their eyes, listen more than you talk, and appreciate any cuddles you get. When you unwind, they will as well.

Chapter 3: Mindful Meditation Explained

It takes a while to explain this concept to people. People believe that when you meditate, the idea is to clear the mind of thoughts, rather than being mindful. They see mindfulness as having thoughts about things and filling the mind with those thoughts. However, that's not what it's about. Mindfulness takes your mind off the trivial and concentrates on the essential. When you learn the difference, you become much more content and can succeed in life because you don't let things such as past and present get in the way of happiness.

Many people try to evade looking at the reality of who they are and prefer to blame their lack of self-awareness on outside stimuli. People who are depressed tell themselves that they have logical reasons to be depressed. People who are too busy in their lives to actually look inside of themselves will blame life for being too busy. It's your choice but the mindfulness path is one that is proven time and time again to make you a much happier person.

The above quotation is very real. You cannot get beyond pain in your life until you break the mold and learn to get beyond it. In mindful meditation practice, you can ease your personal pain because it isn't reinforced by memories of hurtful events or thoughts of things people have said to you. It's all about being in that very moment and that's not where the pain came from. Thus, you allow yourself to move forward without feeling that pain and beginning to actually understand where it came from.

Meditation beginner's exercise

In this first exercise, what we are doing is making you more aware of your body and stilling your mind. This is an exercise that will help you to relax and to put all thoughts of the day out of your mind.

Before you can start real mindful meditation, you need to allow your body to be at ease with itself and this is why this exercise is essential.

Lie down on a comfortable bed or a gym mat making sure that your head is supported and that your neck is comfortable. The neck area takes a lot of stresses and strains especially when you are worried about things. Make sure that your clothing is not constrictive or tight. Place your arms by your side and do not cross your legs. There should be no background music as you need to tune into yourself. You can't do this when you are invaded from outside by sounds or interruptions.

Close your eyes and be aware of your body, starting with your toes and working your way up each part of the body, tensing it and then feeling it drop into a relaxing state. Once that part of the body is completely relaxed, move on to the next part of the body until you have worked your way right up to the top of your head.

Tip: You may find that you are distracted while you are doing this exercise because you are not accustomed to giving your body so much attention. If your thoughts wander, start again. You need to train your mind to tune in with each part of your body. Only when you can do this can you truly feel relaxation.

When the exercise is finished, take your time to open your eyes, sit up slowly and keep the relaxed feeling inside of you.

Exercise 2 – Meditation focusing on breathing

In this exercise, sit up and make sure that your spine is straight. You should just try a comfortable pose. Don't try to sit in common yoga positions. This isn't the aim of the exercise. Place your hands on your lap and move your head to a slightly bowed position as this enhances your breathing. Close your eyes as you do not need outside interference. Put all thoughts out of your mind. The only thought you should have is concentrating on your breathing and the air going in and out of your body. Breathe in through the nose for a count of seven. Hold the breath for the count of four. Breathe out through the mouth, feeling the air coming up from the abdomen to a count of nine. Repeat the exercise 10 times. This will help you to relax. It's a great exercise for any time of day and in any place, but make sure that in the initial stages of mindfulness, you choose somewhere where you will not be distracted by outside influence.

Chapter 4: Who Do You Think You Are?

I want to challenge you on this question and say that you are not your name. You are not your body. You are not your age. You are not the person that has been shaped through the different circumstances you've been through. Here comes the point: You are not your anxiety. One of the first keys to overcoming anxiety is to realize that you are not your thoughts, feelings, and experiences. You are the one who is aware of the thoughts, feelings and different experiences you go through. Depending on how new you are to this idea, this might confuse you. What do I mean you ask? We'll let me guess. You did not buy this book because you wanted information that you can get in almost any bookstore about anxiety. I can tell you that you should change your diet since that could be a part of the problem. You should try natural remedies like essential oils that can help, you should change how you think and begin to have a more realistic approach towards life. All these ideas are great, don't get me wrong. But the purpose of this book is not to repeat all this information that you can get somewhere else.

The purpose of this book is to turn you into what I like to call a warrior of peace. Now once you are a warrior of peace, anxiety won't affect you. You might still have some sensations in your body but you won't label it as anxiety. And to do so, you must adopt more than just positive thinking. You must change your beliefs about who you think you are. I will not recommend that you do affirmations to accomplish this, no we'll go deeper than that.

I want you to detach from everything. Every concept about who you think you are. Even though you probably are a good person with a pleasing personality, I think you can agree with me that something has to change? For me, the pain of remaining the same became too big, and that forced me to change. I keep bringing up change. What change? Clothing style, hair color, relationship, apartment or city type of change? No a change in who you believe you are. Not just an identity shift but a complete detachment from who you think you currently are. If you are serious about overcoming anxiety, then this step is very important.

Have you ever encountered the following scenario? You are about to do something that you know triggers anxiety in you, and you begin to think about how bad it is that the anxiety is coming. All of a sudden it's like you're having anxiety about having anxiety? If you are like me and have experienced this, then that means that the anxiety is too attached to who you think you are. The reason why this happens is because we have too much of an ego-based state of consciousness. If you are not familiar with what the ego is and what it does to us, then I will explain it to you here. Basically, the ego is an illusory sense of self based on one's thoughts and memories. See your ego as a mini person running around in your head and telling you all kinds of things about who you are and what others are and so on. The goal for this mini person running around in your head is to make you believe that he is you. Did you catch that? What this mini person wants you to believe is that HE is YOU. The reason why this mini person wants you to believe this is so that he can begin to create separation between you and the rest of the world.

This mini person or ego can also be called the enemy within. As a warrior of peace, this is the enemy we'll have to conquer. He is one of the biggest reasons for your anxiety and pain. He is the voice inside our head telling us everything that we are. I'm good at this, bad at this, I'm better than this other person, worse than that person, etc. He is the one who does not accept the present moment and wishes for a better time in the future or longs for a time in the past. There is a lot more to this ego, I'm just giving you a brief summary here. Some people who hear this for the first time might ask, What voice inside my head? Or they become angry and denies the voice. This is, of course, the ego speaking and denying.

If this concept is totally new to you, I understand that this can be a little bit overwhelming. Let me point out that everyone has an ego, even the most enlightened people. But they are not attached to it. In the following chapters you'll learn some techniques for how to accomplish this detachment and finally beginning the process of freeing yourself from anxiety.

Key takeaways:

To overcome anxiety you need to detach from your belief of who you think you are currently. Especially if you believe that you are the anxiety or that the anxiety belongs to you.

Become aware of the enemy within (ego) who is constantly trying to force pain into your life by telling you that things should be a different way than it is.

The biggest trick that the enemy within can pull on you is to make you believe that he is you. Knowing this you now have a way of dealing with him. Simply become aware of the thoughts in your head without judging them as good or bad.

Chapter 5: The School Of Zen

Zen is a school of teachings classified as Buddhism's Mahayana. Although Zen stepped out of the shadows, it is still a stream flowing from the Mahayana school of interpretation.

The Mahayana school of thought came into the mainstream 500 years after the original Four Truths were developed. The Mahayana then divided further into different schools over time to include Tibetan Buddhism, Tantric Buddhism and of course, Zen Buddhism.

The Mahayana Buddhism developed teachings that were more inclusive and appealed to a wider swath of society. The inclusivity of the teachings meant that, unlike Theravada teachings, nirvana and enlightenment was something that people from all lifestyles were able to achieve. It was not just meant for the ascetics and monks.

The Beginning of Zen

Zen is the direct translation of the Sanskrit word, Jhana, which means meditation. More importantly, it is a series of steps in the mind's path to evolution and enlightenment. The final step of which is the perfect awareness of all things. Zen emphasizes the role of mindfulness, meditation and combines it with the original Mahayana teaching of compassion and inclusivity.

Zen is rooted in China and dates back to the 6th century after Bodhi dharma exported the teachings to china from India. When it took root in China, it was referred to as the Ch'an School of Buddhism. It arrived in Japan about six centuries later and continued to evolve, being influenced by its new practitioners.

In this version of Buddhism, one was not required to study scripture or sacred teachings. There was no need to worship deities or conduct rituals for one to attain enlightenment. What was needed, instead, was to look inside one's self and attain enlightenment via mindful meditation.

The Essence of Zen

The rationale for the self-enlightenment path is a simple one. They believe that if Siddhartha did it, so can everyone else who truly attempted. In the end, it is one of the truest form of Buddhism because in Buddhism, everyone can attain enlightenment and everyone can become a Bodhi.

However, do not let the simplicity of the procedure cause you to take things lightly or look upon the process callously. The path to enlightenment is hardest when one has to attain it with their own discipline.

Zen training is one of the hardest things, yet one of the most fulfilling. The essence of Zen can be found in the phrase, Vincit Qui Se Vincit, a Latin phrase meaning, 'he who conquers himself conquers the world'. In essence, that is what Zen practices do. In Zen, you conquer yourself and gain the enlightenment of the universe.

Chapter 6: The Power Of Neurotransmitters

In the case described in the last chapter, we saw how releases of dopamine, epinephrine and cortisol among other neurotransmitters could result in the fight or flight response.

But something very similar, albeit much milder also happens when you experience chronic stress. Chronic stress is the kind of stress that 'doesn't go away'. This is not a lion but rather an impending deadline at work, wedding planning, property investment, debt, relationship problems…

This triggers a very similar stress response, which results in continued changes in your body such as suppressed immune function and digestion, a certain amount of tunnel vision, dread and anxiety etc. So when you're stressed for long periods, this negatively affects your ability to relax and to enjoy any experiences – but it also impacts negatively on your health in more ways than you might immediately expect.

Dopamine makes us more driven and focused for instance but only on the thing that is causing the stress. This reduces activity across our brain so that we are more tightly focused on specific thoughts, emotions, ideas and inputs. That's why 'eustress' can actually be a good thing and make you more likely to revise for an exam. But it has also been shown in studies to make us less creative because we're less able to let our mind explore different, diverse ideas.

Likewise, stress also makes it hard for us to focus on anything other than that thing that has our attention.

What's more, is that stress can seriously undermine your ability to impress or influence others. That's because stress is a sign that you're nervous or afraid. If you give of these signs in front of a competitor, then it makes you appear to be less confident and thereby sends the signal that they must be the alpha to your beta. Likewise, if you are anxious when approaching a potential mate, it suggests on an unconscious level that they must be a better potential mate than you – that they are out of your league or at least that you perceive that to be the case!

As you can see then the ability to control your stress response can be a fantastic asset and help you to focus more when you need to, to run faster and to fight harder – or just to appear completely confident and in control in stressful situations.

More Neurotransmitters and What They Do

Conversely, other neurotransmitters can be released in response to pleasure, exercise, sunlight, tiredness, darkness, excitement and more. And these all affect our mood and our ability to focus in other ways.

Serotonin is the neurotransmitter that we think of as the 'happiness hormone'. This is what makes us feel content and happy and it also has a range of other roles such as suppressing pain and decreasing appetite by stimulating the production of leptin.

Melatonin is the neurotransmitter that makes us sleepy!

GABA is an inhibitory neurotransmitter that reduces activity in the brain and can thereby suppress stress and further encourage sleep.

Dopamine is essentially a neurotransmitter that is related to goal-oriented behavior. It makes us more focused and increases memory among other things.

Acetylcholine is one of the principle excitatory neurotransmitters and also plays an important role in memory.

Nitric Oxide is a vasodilator and helps get more blood to the brain and muscles. It also activates neurons that aren't directly connected and thus has an important role in helping us to wake up.

Testosterone is the 'male hormone' that is linked to aggressive thoughts and behaviors as well as drive and confidence.

Estrogen is the female hormone and can have a big impact on mood.

Cortisol is the 'stress hormone' and makes us more alert while creating feelings of dread. It's also linked with appetite, this time making us hungrier via another hormone/neurotransmitter called ghrelin.

Substance P is the neurotransmitter related to the transmission of pain. It also happens to be linked to anger according to some recent research.

Oxytocin, often called the 'love hormone', makes us more agreeable and creates feelings of loving protection and bonding.

Glutamate is another of the most abundant excitatory neurotransmitters and exists in vast quantities compared to any other neurotransmitter.

Anandamide is the 'bliss' neurotransmitter and also appears to stimulate creative thinking.

Once again, these neurotransmitters are released in response to our experiences and thoughts. When a mother sees her child, her brain floods with oxytocin which makes her more likely to bond with the child and feel the need to connect.

When you go on a rollercoaster, your body produces epinephrine and anandamide. When you have just had a great day out, you will be filled with serotonin and feel happy and positive.

In short, your happiness, productivity, creativity, attractiveness, relationships and much more are all responsible for different quantities of these various neurotransmitters.

Neurotransmitters for Incredible Abilities

Certain 'states' can be triggered via the release of specific neurotransmitters and this can be incredibly desirable/positive in some cases.

One example is the much-studied 'flow state'. A flow state is a term for that moment when everything seems to fall into place and you are able to perform at your very best. This results in absolute focus, heightened reactions, improved problem solving and more. It happens when you're snowboarding for instance and the world seems to suddenly slow down, allowing you to pull off incredible moves with expert timing. It also happens when you're so lost in your work that you forget to the toilet or even look up from the computer. And it happens when you talk to a friend all night without realizing how long the conversation has been going. In short, this experience is what total, creative focus feels like. And chemically, it is very similar to the fight or flight response but minus the sensation of fear or dread that normally comes from that. Instead, there seems to be a release of anandamide, which enhances creative problem solving while creating that sense of exhilaration that is so addictive to adrenaline junkies. At the same time, brain scans show that the prefrontal cortex –

the part associated with planning and self-doubt – appears to shut down. This is what removes our sense of time passing and allows us to stay completely fixed on the moment. It's known as 'temporohypofrontality'.

It is thought that all major athletic records were set by flow states and that most highly successful start-ups get to where they get to thanks to flow states.

So imagine if you could trigger a flow state at will and thereby achieve complete focus and perfect problem solving...

The opposite of this state is what's known as the 'default mode network'. This is a network of brain structures that light up when we are completely lost in thought, often while our bodies carry out mundane tasks like showering. This is what allows us to explore diverse regions of our brains and find new connections between ideas – and it's what is believed to have helped Einstein dream up special relativity while working at the patent office.

The 'flashbulb memory' meanwhile shows us how our brains can be capable of laying down much clearer memories during times of extreme shock (such as the moment you heard about 9/11 for instance). Likewise, 'hysterical strength' shows how a strong enough fight or flight response can actually increase muscle fiber recruitment to the point where women have been able to lift cars off of their children trapped underneath.

One underground movement that is interested in the idea of using neurotransmitters to accomplish more is the 'nootropics' movement. Nootropics are 'smart drugs' which tend to work by blocking certain neurotransmitters and encouraging the production of others. These can work like the film 'Limitless' but on a much less powerful scale – slightly increasing memory, focus or even confidence.

The problem with nootropics is that they often come with side effects, haven't been tested in the long term and generally make it harder for us to switch mental state as we need to. It's no good being highly focused if it means your creativity will be suppressed!

Luckily, there are other ways to encourage the production of the correct neurotransmitters to invite the mental states we want...

Chapter 7: Mindfulness-Based Stress Reduction And Mindfulness Exercises

People who practice mindfulness are happier, better, and more successful than those who don't. Those marvelous benefits of practicing mindfulness make you want to practice it yourself. There is a good likelihood you have already tried mindfulness before. Maybe you decided after a few frustrating attempts, that mindfulness isn't for you. However, this is a limiting belief. But like any skill, mindfulness takes practice. So try it again!

In this chapter, you will learn some of the best mindfulness exercises, techniques, and activities to relieve stress and for a better you. We will also learn about what mindfulness-based stress reduction is and how it can help you along your life.

What is Mindfulness Based-Stress Reduction?

Mindfulness-Based Stress Reduction is a plan that teaches you how to relax your mind and body to help you handle stress, anxiety, depression, and sickness.

MBSR focuses on mindfulness, which puts the things happening in the present moment as the primary focus. Mindfulness also is about being aware of your environment, your surroundings, your feelings, your thoughts, and how your body senses. For instance, you may sit silently and remark your emotions. You might only focus on the noises around you or how your food tastes. When you are mindful, you spend close attention to everything you are doing.

By training your mind to focus only on the present, you learn not to get lost in regrets from the past or fretting about the future. Letting go of such thoughts will inevitably help you worry less and accept things as they are. Mindfulness teaches you to be in complete authority of your mind so that your mind doesn't control you.

How Does MBSR work?

To help you concentrate your mind on the current moment, a course in Mindfulness-Based Stress Reduction regularly teaches you to:

Focus your attention on your entire body, from head to toe. With body scan, you will notice the places where you feel tense or pain. You might see how your stomach rises and falls as you exhale.

Focus on the thoughts that move through your mind, but don't judge them. For instance, you might notice that thoughts concerning works enter your mind. Instead of worrying about work, only record the thought and feeling without worrying about them.

Then, return your attention back to the present moment. It is common for the mind to ramble when a person starts to exercise mindfulness. If that happens, it's alright. This is the reason why mindfulness is a practice - it takes consistent practice to not judge your emotions and thoughts.

It takes practice to live in the present moment. You will need to practice yoga, breathing exercises, stretches, and poses to strengthen the mind and relax the muscles. With all this being said, we will now discover more ways to practice mindfulness.

Avoid Multitasking

Many people believe that multitasking increases productivity. However, multitasking is only doing several things at once, with very poor quality. Most of all it holds you from taking advantage of the present moment. When you multitask, your focus will be all over the place, instead of focusing what you're doing at the present moment. Multitasking allows your mind to straggle from one task to another. It is not productive or beneficial.

For instance, if you are talking with a colleague and at the same time you are checking social media, you lose the precious experience of bonding with another person. Whenever you are working, look for assignments that need the utmost attention. Prioritize these tasks until you finish them all off. Once you are done with one task, move on to the next.

When you are going out with your buddies, give your undivided attention to your friends, the activities, and your surroundings. Take full advantage of the experience and appreciate your time with them. Have fun at the moment that you are together. Do not procrastinate and check your emails, phone calls, and other trivialities. Make the most of each moment spent with your loved ones; you might not get another chance.

When you stop multitasking, you finish one job faster with better quality. It also places you far away from the pitfall of being overwhelmed and stressed out. When you multitask and work on numerous of things, chances are you are not going to finish anything. Your tasks will stack up, and before you know it, you are overwhelmed. If you give priority to the most important tasks and organize your workload, your duties will become much easier.

Spend Time with Yourself

In today's regular connected world, finding isolation has become a lost caused. When you spend time with yourself, it will be much to your advantage. It's easy to get lost in this lively world; you may have a variety of things to do, either work-related, school-related, family-related, etc. To exercise mindfulness in one of the best ways, grab a cup of coffee and spend a couple of minutes sitting down doing nothing. You can practice this during lunchtime, after work, or before you fall asleep.

So many people are so caught up with life. They are very stressed and overwhelmed with plenty of things. They need a break, but they are confused on how. All you need is to spend five to ten minutes alone every day. Find a quiet spot where you could relax your mind and body. Set down everything that is bothering you. Do not think about anything whether it's your job or family.

Ignore your bills and even the goals you want to reach soon. Rather, solely focus on your breathing. Take notice of your surroundings. Enjoy the time you are giving yourself. Be careful of your thoughts; they can throw your focus off balance, which may ruin the mood. The second you think about any of your problems or any other distracting thoughts, put your focus back on your breathing.

Spend time on yourself and remain quiet and relaxed for as long as you want. You will feel as though a heavy burden is lifting off from your shoulders. It means you are now living in the present moment. Despite your hectic schedule, always find time to be alone and spend time with yourself.

Be Optimistic

Always believe that everything will turn out for the best! When you hold a positive viewpoint on life, two things will happen. First, you will not be scared anymore of all the wrong things that occurred in your past. You will just sweep them aside and let them vanish from your memory. Second, you will no longer be concerned about what will happen to you the following day.

Because you are in a healthy condition, you will be able to relieve yourself from past failures and future problems. If you are optimistic, you can put your energy on what is happening at this very moment, which is the most important thing. However, not a lot of people can do that because they are living in a negative and pessimistic state of mind. Some are troubled by their past; others are too watchful of their future. Do your best to avoid being in that negative mood.

To live in the moment, you must do anything that fascinates you. Do not try to satisfy anyone, but yourself. Many people are always thinking about what others will say about them. Therefore, they never live in the moment and truly be themselves. Don't live your life following other people's opinions. Live as though nothing cares about what you do. Live in the world where judgment does not exist. Live in the world where only you make the rules.

Focus on the things that you desire to do, regardless of what others would say about it. Nevertheless, it is your life that you are living and not theirs. Starting today, you need to have a positive outlook on life. You must become optimistic. You shouldn't let others control what you do. Live in the moment and enjoy things of today, especially the things that you have missed due to fear and self-consciousness.

Love What You Do

In life, you have to make sure that you like what you are doing. You must love your work and everything you do. Sadly, there's not a lot of people that can speak positively about their careers. Most will say they stay at their jobs because they have things to buy, bills to pay and to provide for everything else. However, they feel terrible about what they do. Doing something that you don't like and sticking with negative friends will only infuriate your pain and misery, especially in the long run.

When you feel unmotivated at work, it will take a toll on your performance. You will work late and won't finish your tasks by the assigned deadline, and you will have a tense relationship with your boss. If you dislike your job, an ideal thing to do is to look for another. Try to recognize the things that you need to do and the stuff that you don't like. This way, you can quickly find a new job that suits your enthusiasm. Be sure to get a job that doesn't relate to your former position. This way you are sure to experience new things.

Finding a new interest or career will not be easy. It is possible that you might now settle for the job you want. So, it will be for the best that you highlight the things you like from the past. Focus on the positive features and magnify those factors as much as you can. Do your best to put your view away from the things you loathe. This way at least you will have something to look forward to every time you go to work. When the opportunity arises, and you get a job that you like, that is the only time to leave. Most of the time it takes patience and a strong effort to achieve what you want in life.

Learn the Art of Acceptance

In life, there are some things that you cannot control and change, and you must accept that. Lots of people struggle in life because they keep going after things that are beyond their reach. They are overwhelmed with the stuff that they cannot manage. Most importantly, it will also teach you how to accept things that are way beyond your control. To live in the present, to live life to the fullest, you must learn the art of acceptance.

It is a powerful tool that only a small portion of people exercise. Acceptance is tough because it goes against your pride. If you got dumped by your boyfriend/girlfriend, it would hurt your self-esteem. You might become angry or anxious about how other people see you and become doubtful of many other relationships. However, this is not true. You should accept that the fact that your partner doesn't care about you and move on to find a better partner.

Everybody wants to take control and change everything to their liking. However, you cannot change everybody and everything. But you can accept things and appreciate them for what they are.

Accepting People

In life, you have to live with people that might go against everything you stand for. It's this differentness that makes life exciting. Do not try to change people you don't like. If your best friend acts a certain way, do not tell them to behave in a particular manner, simply because it doesn't accommodate you. If your partner is sensitive, do not urge her to be more logical. It's who they are. After all, you would not want another person telling you to change something about yourself. Rather than trying to change who they are and become frustrated by the outcome, try to embrace them and appreciate everything about them. When you start to see the positive in everybody, you will realize that acceptance is quite easy.

Accepting Difficult Situations

When people are confronted with a stressful situation, their typical reaction is to panic and do anything it takes to move away from it. But, escaping from your problems will not solve anything. It will only make the situation worse. Whenever you find yourself in a desperate circumstance, don't try to escape. Rather, take a mindful breath, stay calm, and accept that today is not your day. When you have complete acceptance of your circumstance, it will be much easier for you to look for ways to bounce back.

Start Your Day with Something Positive

Whether you realize it or not, rising every morning to the ringing of your alarm clock will not be the best moment of your day. There are plenty of times when you had to haul yourself out of bed and hurry your way to work or school. The way you begin your morning will set the course for the rest of the day. When you start your morning irritated, cynical, or overwhelmed, you are going to have a tough time feeling the positive vibes of the day.

Therefore, always start your day with an upbeat attitude and anticipate all the good things that will happen. To live positively, you must believe that everything will work out for the best. You can start by just acknowledging your morning with a smile and be grateful that you are still breathing and your body parts are all there. When you do that, it will set the positive feeling for the entire day.

It is essential for you to be positive despite all the wrong things that are befalling. Doing so helps distract your attention. It allows you to concentrate more on the bright side rather than the dark side. After you start your morning with something positive, do not just leave the positive attitude and energy at your bed. Take it with you as you head to work or wherever you are going for the day.

Welcome everyone with a smile and positivity. When you do this, people will see you like a sympathetic, generous, and happy person. Moreover, it will make everyone else feel good. So, the next time you catch your alarm clock ringing, don't get discouraged that you need to wake up. Rather, be grateful that you can hear and be thankful that you woke up today.

Declare it to yourself that there is a beautiful day waiting for you.

Start your morning with a positive outlook and always bring that with you. Be free enough to share this positive affection with others by simply welcoming and smiling at them. Always believe that there is a great wonderment expecting for you along the way. Do not forget to smile and stay happy. And keep on practicing this until it is your habit.

Show Love for Everything!

One of the most powerful tools that you can use to enjoy the excellence of the present moment and that life brings is to give love to all that surrounds you. Never be afraid to pour your heart out in everything that you do. Do it with heartfelt passion and intensity. Do things with love and desire.

Random Acts of Kindness

Make it a practice of doing good things every day. It does not have to be overboard. A mere act of kindness, to make someone feel good about their day is enough. You can do it by bringing in donuts for the office. Or you can make a note of appreciation for your boss or colleagues.

You can also say thank you to the people who opened the door for you. Make it a part of your daily routine to do good things to others. When you approach others with love and respect, you would also feel good about yourself. Furthermore, you will realize that you are capable of spreading such love and kindness.

Breathing

Breathing is one of the best exercises you can use to reduce stress. When you are under stress, your chest feels tense, and you breathe fast and shallow. This is a natural response to danger or stressful situation. However, conscious breathing exercises is an effective way to reduce stress. When you inhale and exhale, focus on keeping your chest still while opening and closing your stomach. Take a few minutes of your day to breathe until you enter a state of relaxation and calmness.

Love what you do

Whether you are completing a project to meet a fixed deadline or merely washing the dishes, try to see the benevolence in all that you do. If you establish love and passion in everything you are doing, everything will become clearer to finish. Therefore, the next time you find yourself stressed out because of a particular project, lie back and take a mindful deep breath.

Try to envision how valuable it will be for you to be able to finish the project by a given deadline. You will be more motivated about your goals rather than discouraged.

Love Yourself

If you want to be truly happy, you must love yourself. You cannot notice the value of life if you cannot give yourself love and appreciation.

Do not be too hard on yourself. Stop criticizing yourself for all the faults and failures that you encountered in the past. Take pride in all your accomplishments, whether big or small. Above all, spend time with people who truly brings the best of you.

Mindful Eating

Mindful eating is a powerful way to practice mindfulness If you can make sure that you are eating mindfully, you can exercise mindfulness with every meal. This change to your eating regime will make a vast difference in your life. Practicing mindfulness while at the same time diet and become healthier. Think about it for a second. You can lose weight by being more mindful of what you eat? Try it the next time you enjoy a meal. Mindful eating is also a fantastic approach to enjoy your food even more. It encourages you to focus and enjoy it. You will regard how your food tastes and how you like them. If you are mindful about the way you eat, you can stop cravings and other problems. Mindfulness encourages you to acknowledge cravings without any judgment and with the understanding that they will dwindle. You may crave a sweet dessert, but mindfulness encourages you to know that if you do not get your dessert, your cravings will die down. Here are some necessary steps to mindful eating:

- Modify your diet. Think about the health of each ingredient you add to your diet and add it to your shopping list. This will help you avoid unnecessary items when you shop. Avoid all processed foods, sodas, alcohol, and any other unhealthy foods that may damage your health.

- Be mindful of when your stomach tells you that it is time to eat. Listen to your stomach, rather than your cravings. Be patient and avoid overeating as much as you can.

- Start with a small portion of food and continue to eat until your stomach is full.

- Appreciate your food to your heart content. Take a minute to pause before you begin enjoying your meal. Express your gratitude for the opportunity to enjoy tasty food and the people you are eating and enjoying it with.

- Use all your senses to whatever you are eating. When you are cooking, serving, and eating food, take notice to the texture, color, scent, and even flavor of the different foods you make.

- Eat slowly and chew thoroughly. It is easier to taste food completely when you eat your food and enjoy all the flavors of the meal.

Make use of these mindful steps that can bring a whole new light to the way you are eating. You will enjoy the food you are eating more. It will be easier for your body to tell you when you are full and when you should stop eating. You may find that mindful eating makes you feel empowered and enjoy the time you spend eating more. Mindful eating gives you the chance to control your inclinations and avoid overeating. Not only that, but if you are eating it, you will not have cravings for unhealthy foods, but rather have cravings for foods which give you the energy to enjoy them more.

Chapter 8: Techniques To Develop The Mindful Kid

Let's face it, the idea of your kid sitting quietly and focusing on his breath for extended periods, just, is not going to happen. Zero fun. But, what if you could teach your child a variety of games that require him or her to focus their attention?

A bit of a sidebar here. My experience is that video or computer games are the crack-cocaine of youth entertainment. My kids love cards and a host of other great board games. But, frankly, they can't compete with computer games. So, I have had to wean my kids off gaming as much as possible. It's tough, but the research supports my very unpopular stance with my kids. The good news is that after a week of screen time prohibition, my kids stop asking for it and fill in the time with other, more creative and interactive activities.

You can do these games with one child or more.

Mindfulness Meditation - Kid Style

To teach your child 'how to mindfully focus' on his or her breath...

Sit in a Quiet Peaceful Room: To begin, choose a quiet, serene place that helps the two of you focus on your breathing movements easily. You could sit outdoors, but make sure to select an area that isn't noisy. This way, you'll be able to concentrate on your breath.

Give your child a cushion to sit on if sitting on the floor is difficult or uncomfortable for him or her. Ask your child to either cross his or her legs or keep them straight extending forward. Next, ask the child to focus on their breathing as you learned in the last chapter.

Focusing on their breathing can be a little difficult for children since they aren't used to focus on something for long. However, the helpful tricks below can assist your child to become mindful of their breathing and bodily movements with a lot of ease.

Tips To Help Your Child Become More Mindful

Set the mood. Unless you like to make things amazingly difficult, don't start a mindfulness meditation session with your child (at any age) when they feel distressed, super hyper, hungry, or sick. If you can, pick a spot during their normal down time when there is peak calmness.

Prime the pump. OK, to help settle a child before a mindfulness session, start with an activity that is calming. For example, before I sit down with my two little whirling dervishes to meditate for say 5 minutes, I'll have them read on their own, solve a sudoku puzzle, paint or draw for 20 minutes. I give them so much latitude on this; just as long as it does not involve any screen or it doesn't get their heart rate above 100 beats per minute.

Ask the child to practice with their breathing buddy: A breathing buddy is a toy, preferably a stuffed animal that your child can use while practicing mindfulness breathing. Props can pique your child's curiosity and make your sessions more enjoyable.

Ask the child to lie flat on their back on an exercise mat and place their breathing buddy on the top of their belly. Now, ask them to take deep breaths and focus on how their buddy moves upwards and downwards with the motion of their belly. This will certainly excite your child because most children enjoy new exercises and techniques.

Tell your child that he or she must focus on how their breath 'swings' their buddy and if they become distracted, they should think of their stuffed toy. Practice this for about seven to ten minutes, or even for longer if the child does not become bored. A daily ten-minute practice is sufficient to help your child become familiar with mindfulness.

Place Hands on Belly: When you ask your child to lie down as a means to practice mindfulness meditation, ask him or her to gently place his or her hands on their belly and notice how their belly rises and falls with each inhalation and exhalation. This will be a fun-filled activity for your child and will accompany lots of chuckles and giggles.

Don't rebuke the child if he or she finds it too amusing and cannot control the giggling and laughter. Instead, laugh with them and enjoy the moment. Once, their laughter subsides and they no longer find it hilarious, sweetly ask them to focus on their belly's movements and their breathing.

Inquire About Their Feelings: Once the meditation session is over, ask your child how he or she feels and what they experienced. Find out if he or she felt more connected with their body and could feel every tiny movement that occurred in their body while they were breathing. This small discussion will help your child better understand the goal he or she is trying to achieve. The next time you practice mindfulness breathing together, your child will know what he or she wants to accomplish and can do a better job.

You should also find out if your child experienced any discomfort or troubling emotions during the practice. Use this practice as a way to bond with your child and find out the thoughts going on in his or her mind so you can change them with the help of mindfulness.

In the next chapter, we'll look at how to cultivate attention in children by helping them develop, nurture, and exercise their "attention muscle". This is a fantastic expression. If you can imagine that paying attention requires a muscle to do it, then paying attention to the things you want to pay attention to gets stronger with exercise.

Training Your Child's "Attention Muscles"

Once you've familiarized your child to mindful breathing, you can expand these sessions by teaching him how to become mindful of their entire body.

Most children find it hard to focus on something for long. Often, when children discover something new and exciting, their attention on that thing or experience does not last long before the child loses interest. This is healthy and normal during the early childhood development and experts state that children aged between two and six can only focus on something for about 4 to 20 minutes.

How to Train your Child's Attention Muscle

Let us look at techniques you can apply to develop your child's attention muscle, and in the process, increase his or her attention span, concentration, and alertness.

To train your child's attention muscle, we first need to ignite the flame of curiosity. Children rarely enjoy the same activity or exercise if it becomes repetitive. Therefore, try something different from the 'breathing buddy' and 'hands on belly' techniques to enhance your child's attention span and focus.

Below are alternate mindfulness exercises guaranteed to spark curiosity in your little one.

Mindful Eating

Mindfulness in eating is an interesting activity that can train your child to become more attentive in an easy, fun way. When you sit together for a meal, tell your child that you are going to add a little excitement to the meal by changing it into a game.

Tell your child to take a few deep breaths and then ask him to eat their meal one bite at a time. Each bite of food is on its own journey from the plate to the fork to the mouth, down the throat and finally into the belly. Instruct the child to chew each bite very slowly and feel the texture, aroma, and flavor of the bite. When chewing a bite, the child must focus on the chewing action only and must not make another bite. If the child wants a drink, he must wait until the food has made its way to his stomach.

This simple practice will make your child curious about his or her food and will start asking you questions. Answer them, but make sure not to speak when the child is chewing or taking a bite.

Add a competitive twist to the game by tracking how many bites your child pays attention to. If they are old enough, provide them with a pencil and paper to track it themselves. If they get to 15 full attention bites, offer them a reward of your choosing. My kids are keen for anything with chocolate, so that's usually a good incentive for them. Focusing on each bite not only helps to build their attention muscle, it makes them slow down their eating to mark down their score (there are all sorts of digestive health benefits for slower, mindful eating). This exercise also calls attention to their personal integrity. Are they marking down a mindful bite when it's not a mindful bite? With humor and grace, these can be marvelous opportunities to set your bundles of joy down the right path.

Mindful Painting

Tell your child you need him to create a beautiful painting with his bare hands. Offer your child different color paints and ask him to dip his fingers into the colors and paint anything on the paper. Before the child paints, ask the child to take five mindful breaths and then start painting.

Have your child focus on how the paint feels on his fingers, to experience the feeling of running 'paint-dripping-wet hands' on a canvas or paper; coax him into experiencing the sense, touch and feel of the activity.

Ask the child to take another five breaths after ten minutes and continue with this practice for as long as they enjoy it. You can try the same exercise with building sandcastles, building structures with Legos, or any other activity that involves the use of hands. The idea is to help your child experience different textures and surfaces so they become mindful of their sense of touch and can use it to enhance their ability to focus on things.

Treasure Hunt

Plan a treasure hunt. Hide some toys in the backyard, garden, or a room in your house. If she is old enough, provide your daughter with a checklist of items to be ticked off when it has been found. If she's not old enough, start with a small number of her most memorable stuffed toys. Provide your daughter with a bag to collect the items. A reusable shopping bag works great.

Once the items have been collected, and you have congratulated your young Sherlock Holmes, have them sit down, close their eyes and reach into the bag and describe each item.

As your child grows and develops, he or she is bound to experience mixed feelings as he or she interacts with a new world, friends, environment, etc. In the next chapter of our mindfulness for children blueprint, we are going to outline how children and parents can use mindfulness as an effective tool to manage new and difficult feelings.

Coping with Difficult Emotions

Mindfulness helps you become calm, relaxed, and composed. The daily practice of being aware of your thoughts, emotions, and feelings has the natural by-product of paying attention to your own raw emotions instead of stewing in them and being subjected to their direct influence. It's almost like watching a person being angry, for example, instead of being angry yourself. You are not feeling the intensity of what he is feeling.

Imagine having the skill to take a fly on the wall perspective of your own self. It's hard to stay in the intensity of difficult emotions if you just plainly observe them.

By now, I'm likely preaching to the choir: teach your child how to use mindfulness to calm the mind when it's troubled.

No Bull Shit here. You'll have your work cut out for you. Kids, especially as they get older are not keen to share their feelings. However, the following mindful techniques will help your kid achieve more peace and build up trust with you in the process. You may find that it opens the lines of communication for healthy dialogue.

Focusing Inwards: Children Mindfulness Techniques for Handling Emotions, Feelings, and Internal Thoughts

Below are techniques you can use to teach your child how to be mindful of his or her feelings, emotions, and thoughts, and build his or her capacity to handle these emotions irrespective of their nature.

The Super Hero Mindfulness Game

Almost every child loves superheroes, be it Spiderman, Batman, Flash, Hulk, Wonder Woman, or Captain America. If she's younger, maybe that hero is Dora, the Explorer or Thomas, the Tank Engine. I'm sure you already know without asking. Your kid's lunch box or bed sheets are covered with its image. You can leverage her connection to this superhero to help your child become aware of his or her complicated feelings. Once there is awareness, she can better recognize these feelings, thoughts, and emotions and breathe them down.

Ask your child to play with you and bring his superhero figurine along. Tell your child you want to teach him or her a trick that will make them strong and powerful like their beloved superhero. Then, ask the child to take five or six deep breaths and imagine that they are the superhero.

If your son likes Batman, tell him to imagine that he is the real Batman. Now, ask him to close his eyes, focus on what it might be like at home, school or at sporting events as that superhero. Allow this fantasy to play out for a few minutes.

Now, ask him to think about being that same superhero again, only this time, ask your son to imagine having to overcome conflict or a difficult task. Let him think on this for a few more minutes then ask him to open his eyes. Ask him about his thoughts and if he discovered any intense feelings. If the answer is yes, take interest in his thoughts and feelings and ask more questions but don't sound pushy. Once you know the thoughts bothering him, tell him to look for its solution as his superhero does. He might come to his own conclusion to handle the situation with courage and confidence.

Practice the exercise at least once a week to understand the different thoughts and feelings your child is experiencing and guide him or her to resolve them effectively.

The Personal Weather Report Mindfulness Game

When you have a calm moment with your daughter, ask her to use the weather to describe how she is feeling (describe their mood). Give the child different weather options, such as windy, calm, rainy, tsunami, stormy, and sunny.

Ask your child to choose a weather condition that describes her mood, emotional state, or feelings at that very moment. This will prompt the child to think about his or her thoughts and emotions for a while and understand his or her current emotional state.

When the child gives you an answer, tell him or her that nobody can modify the weather outside, but everyone, including your child, can certainly change his or her inner weather. When a child learns this, it will help the child become more peaceful.

If she chooses windy or stormy, gently, ask her why she feels that way.

She might become a little overwhelmed; if you need calm immediately, ask her to identify 5 red (color doesn't matter) objects in the area. Just that simple thoughtful task will help. Once she's a little calmer, ask her to focus on 5 breaths at her belly. Once the fear ebbs, continue exploring the reasons behind her mood. Don't force it. If it's too difficult for her to talk, give it time. After a handful of these moments, she will confide in you. She is beginning to understand that your intentions are not to criticize or to punish, but they are to help her navigate through rough waters.

Return to paying attention to the breath. Ask her to close her eyes and imagine having the power to place the bad weather in a big soap bubble and letting a gentle breeze blow it away. With each returning difficult feeling, ask her to imagine the bad feeling is a storm cloud in her stomach and she has the power to move it from her stomach to the inside of the soap bubble. Let her imagine it drifting away in the breeze. What's left in her stomach (where many of us hold tension) is the beautiful clear sunny sky.

Carry out these practices as many times as possible to help your child become aware of negative feelings and thoughts so he or she can learn how to manage them better.

The Counting Pyramid

Not to generalize, but often boys are more difficult to keep still. I offer a technique to those of you with competitive, restless boys & girls. The counting pyramid works like this.

Ask you kid to imagine a pyramid with steps. Start with an easy task; imagine a pyramid with 5 steps up and 5 steps down.

Now ask him to close his eyes. For each breath, he will climb one step in his minds eye: breathe - step 1: breathe - step 2: breathe - step3 and so on. Once he gets to the top, step 5, he comes down taking an imaginary step down with each breath 4, 3, 2, 1.

If he loses is place when his mind wanders, ask him to go back to the last step he remembers and to finish his journey.

Now 5 steps to the top is pretty easy...but the more steps, the more difficult it is to maintain focus or mindfulness. I like to have competitions with my son (we typically choose 50 steps)- certainly, the competition is not how fast you can climb up and down the pyramid...slower breathing is preferred actually. But, our competition is more to do with how many times we lose our place and have to go back to the stair we last remember counting.

Your kid might find it easier not to lose her place if she imprints the number in her mind with bright white or funky colors right on the pyramid steps.

Unburden the Young Mind

Mindfulness means to be open and curious about your present moment experience. It means to accept what you experience as it is without leaving the moment to fret about the past or worry about the future.

When you learn to live in the present, you are able to curb the storm of negative emotions erupting inside you. You observe the thoughts and emotions behind that storm and you will more effectively manage it.

This is exactly what you need to teach your kids so that they, too, can better regulate through difficult times.

For most children, childhood years are full of fun, play, excitement, enthusiasm, and love. But all children will suffer hardship; this is normal. And as difficult as this is for you, it is helpful for them to experience moderate hardship. In fact, these are critical life skills best learned at a young age.

In some cases, the hardship is not moderate. It is vile with long lasting implications. It may include bullying, verbal abuse, sexual harassment, neglect by a parent and more.

As much as we want to protect our kids with our mama bear instincts, we still need to teach our kids how to self-manage the negative emotions; that strife without coping skills can lead children down the wrong path.

Inner Peace: Mindfulness Techniques for Quelling the Inner Storms

The Past Doesn't Last

When your child is practicing a mindfulness meditation session with you, tell him that today you want to talk about the importance of letting go of past mistakes or troubles, and become more aware of the present.

Coax him into believing the past is just that, history, and it's the present moment that is most dear. If your child finds it difficult to understand, just ask him or her to breathe and think of the traumatic episode that has shattered him. Let him know he is safe right now and draw from him a small list of the blessings he has.

It's natural that he will return to his worry. Ask him to think about his favorite book or TV show. Tell him that the main character of this story wants to talk to him about his worries. Let him know that the character wants to write a book or make a TV show about his worry; during the new story, the main character destroys the worry and takes your son on the most fantastic journey EVER.

Instruct your child to imagine this character will stop whatever he's doing to help your child whenever he or she feels confused, disturbed, or annoyed.

Chapter 9: Creating Healthy Relationships

Human beings are conditioned to establish relationships for mutual benefit. When you choose to live alone, you will needlessly carry a lot of burdens. But establishing relationships is not as easy or smooth as it may first seem. First off, you have to have an understanding of the type of people that you can get along with. Find those people and then approach them with your proposition. In reality, it seems like a flow, but you have to prepare mentally so that you are not misled. Relationships are very important — unless they stop being healthy. By becoming regular practitioners of mindfulness, we train ourselves to be the best relationship candidates by putting a shine to our good qualities and minimizing or getting rid of our negative traits. The following are some of the ingredients of a healthy relationship.

Mutual respect

Whether it's a business or romantic relationship, the parties must have respect for one another. When either or both parties have little or no respect for one another, the relationship is most probably going to be abusive and the end results will be nasty. Respect can be detected in the manner you treat your partner and what you say to them when they are not around. Fake respect doesn't count because it eventually rears its ugly face, causing bitterness and resentment.

Trust

In a relationship, you have to trust your partner and your partner has to trust you. Under normal circumstances, humans are slow to trust because they fear that you might be another person that wants to do them in. Trust is earned. If you encounter someone who has trust issues, don't immediately distance yourself from them —just give them time. However, you can only wait so long. The easiest way to earn your partner's trust is to act consistently in their best interests. In other words, be loyal.

Honesty

Honesty counts for a lot. Some people think that honesty should be expected of the big affairs only. Wrong! If you're dishonest in small affairs, you will also be dishonest in big affairs. A relationship that is founded on honest terms and whose partners continue to practice honesty is bound to be long and fruitful. On the other hand, a relationship where one party or all parties are dishonest will meet a fiery end. When a relationship works, it will bring out the best in us, but if it doesn't work, it could potentially pit the former partners into the worst rivals ever!

Compromise

Sometimes you will not feel like doing something, but in light of your partner's needs, you will be forced to do it anyway and the vice-versa is true. Being interested in taking compromises will improve the health of your relationship. But if you're vicious, uncooperative, and strong-willed, you risk losing your partner. If you and your partner are embroiled in a fight and are trying to work out a solution, you should both agree to let go of the hard bargaining and find a common ground.

Individuality

In the case of long-term relationships, you may find the partners becoming alike in both manners and looks. Although this might sound like a sweet idea, it never is. When two people are very much alike and share the same living space, the initial amusement will wear off and in its place, contempt and detest will take over. In order for parties to a relationship to stay in awe of one another, they must each maintain their individuality. An ideal relationship is one where the partners have no satisfaction of having figured out one another.

Good communication

Nothing spells doom to a relationship faster than poor communication. Partners must always be in talking terms and the most important things must be always talked about. When you hold something back from your partner, they will instinctively know it and begin to question your authenticity. Good communication indicates that your relationship is healthy. But in order to get there, you have to put in the work and cultivate a communication style that appeals to both partners.

Control of negative emotions

Most husbands say that they are terrified of what's going to come out of their wife's mouth when they are angered. Humans hardly forget a terrible word that was uttered to them. But the only thing that can turn this around is developing control of negative emotions. With enough practice, you can master your emotions to the point that you could be brewing with anger and yet not let it show through verbal abuse. It is also critical to develop control of your negative emotions so that you can be able to fight fair. Partners shouldn't be ruthless to one another. Nothing incites resentment in a person more than enduring cruelty at the hands of their partner.

Humility

Every relationship has its rules, but the one rule that works wonders in every relationship is humility. Some people tend to hold themselves from being humble thinking that people will consider them weak. Actually, in a world full of narcissists and charlatans, humility is a strength, not weakness. When you present yourself to your partner as a humble person, you will endear yourself to them and they are likely to return the favor. But when you move around with an air of superiority, you will cause them to despise you and want to do you harm.

Intimacy

A relationship devoid of intimacy is an ailing relationship. But there's no one way of doing it. Intimacy can run along the philosophy that you both agree upon. But it must have a ritualistic element.

Patience

Never demand your partner to move at your pace. If they are too slow or too fast for your liking, perhaps it's time you went back to weighing their advantages and disadvantages and ultimately decide whether or not they are worth the trouble.

Chapter 10: Beginning Mindful Meditation

We title this chapter as the beginning of mindful meditation and not beginning mindfulness, because the two are intertwined. Mindfulness is the soul of meditation, and meditation is the outward grace of mindfulness. Mindfulness can exist without meditation, but meditation cannot exist without mindfulness.

There are ten steps a layperson needs to discover the power of mindful meditation.

Step One

Sit in a room that is void of all distraction. This is important in the first stage. As much as possible, there should be no sound, no aroma (good or bad), no light. There should be nothing that triggers any of your five senses other than the point where your skin touches the place where you sit.

Sit in a position that keeps your torso uninhibited so that breathing is as natural and as easily accomplished as possible. If you have a reclining chair, you can use that, or if you would like to sit on the floor, place a cushion and situate yourself on that cushion.

Close your eyes and begin the exercise by mentally locating your toes. See your feet and your toes, then breathe in consciously and breathe out. As you breathe out, release any muscle tension in your toes. Next move to your calf muscles, which are a point of great distraction and tension and do the same. Locate it, breathe in, and relax while you exhale. You may need to do this a two or three times. Next are your thighs, followed by your pelvic floor then your lower back followed by your palms, your arms and then your shoulder and neck. By the time you get to this, your body should be in total relaxation.

Lastly do the same to your facial muscles. All expression should be wiped away and once you feel your face relaxed, pull your lips in a mild smile till you actually feel the face relax more, then stop the smile there. Your face, in its most relaxed position is actually a smile. I call it the Buddha smile. You see the same facial expression on most Buddha statues.

Step one is now complete.

Step Two

Once you are in this position, turn your attention to your breathing. Do not control your breathing. Do not speed up or slow it down, merely observe it. The breathing, at this point, is controlled by a part of your brain. It is not you controlling it. You can observe it. As you watch your breath, you will notice that its depth changes over time, sometimes you will even notice its frequency will change. Let it change. Just watch.

Step Three

You are not meditating, at this point you are being mindful of just one thing - your breathing. But our minds are not static and thoughts will appear. You will feel an array of other thoughts pervade your state at this point. The key is not to fight it. The key is to let it come and pass. Just as we mentioned the analogy of the passing car. Let the thought flow through. However, instead of shunning the thought and getting frustrated that you are being bothered by it, I want you to watch that thought. Look at it without interacting with it and judging it. Accept that thought for what it is - pure energy. Remember—do not interact with it. Interacting with a thought is like stepping away from the curb while you were watching the stream of cars, stepping into the street and trying to stop the car. Don't do that. Learn to watch the thought go by.

Step Four

Each time a thought penetrates your stillness and you've let it pass without sulking and judging; you will get used to the concept that you are not required to interact with every thought that comes your way. As you practice this more over the course of your life, you will find that it becomes easier. It will become so easy that you will begin to feel your consciousness peel away from the rest of your brain and mind.

Just as a side note, you must remember that the brain holds your memories. There is a physical location to your memories. Science has given us the ability to locate and pinpoint the exact location of different abilities in the brain, including memory. One of the greatest confusions than man lives under is the notion that the brain and the consciousness are co-located. They are not.

The breathing exercises and mindfulness practice that you are now going through will slowly bring you to the realization that you can peel your consciousness away from the other functions of your brain. You can do this up to the point that you can watch everything else go by. When you can do this, you are getting to the point of true mindfulness.

Step Five

Each time thoughts pervade, bring yourself back gently to monitoring your breath. Keep focusing on your breath. As you keep doing this, you will find that your sessions get longer. From the first time you do this, never keep track of time with it. Do not set a clock and say, 'I will meditate for 30 minutes today". Do not do that. Let your experience build naturally. If you are distracted, and you would like to start again, you may do so. You can restart the exercise as many times as you like in each sitting. The only requirement is that you do not allow exasperation or expectation to set in.

Step Six

When you naturally exit the state of mindfulness, you can choose to re-enter or end your session for the evening.

Chapter 11: How Meditative Practices "Rewire" Your Brain

For centuries, practitioners of meditation have argued that the practice has completely changed their life. Their perception of reality, and even their nature of the "I." In this chapter, I discuss how modern neuroscience helps to look at these statements from a new angle, and how this knowledge can enrich our practice and all of life in general.

Meditation practitioners seek truth through careful study of their inner, subjective experience. Some call it "first-person research." Science looks at the external material world and relies on third-party research and objective methodology. As a result of discoveries made in this way, any other scientist can check and repeat.

Scientists have traditionally considered the claims of practitioners of meditation with healthy skepticism. And meditation practitioners reciprocated them and with the same skepticism, treated the demands of scientists to provide objective evidence that meditation is beneficial. Hence, the National Institute of Health allocated funding to several research projects devoted to the effects of meditation on a person. Other studies examine the effects of the practice of mindfulness and meditative techniques in general on human health and the possibilities of self-healing of the body. Neuroscientists have identified thousands of practitioners of meditation. From novice citizens to monks from Tibetan monasteries, changes in brain activity compared to those who do not meditate.

Of course, you can succeed in practice, and without understanding what is happening with your brain at this moment. And certainly without the beautiful scans obtained with an MRI. On the other hand, modern science offers us to look at our practice. And our life as a whole. From a new angle, and this can be not only extremely interesting but also quite important.

So, is it possible with the help of modern scientific methods to find out what meditation practitioners have been saying for centuries? That a meditator becomes calmer, that his stress level decreases, that he begins to manage his attention better? And is it possible to detect real neuronal changes corresponding to these changes in the practitioner's subjective experience?

Over the past few decades, we have a huge amount of evidence that the human body and mind are inextricably linked. It turned out that we can literally change ourselves and our perception of the world through meditation. By learning to focus our attention differently in the practice of concentration and the practice of open presence, we can directly influence the work of the various systems of our brain that control our attention.

Changes in Different Parts of the Brain

One of the most interesting areas of research is the study of how the practice of meditation can physically change the structure of the brain. Immediately, several neuroscientists have shown in their works that some areas of the brain for those who regularly practice meditation are physically different from those of the non-practitioners. Moreover, these changes occur already during the first eight weeks of regular practice.

The practice of meditation physically changes the structure of areas of the brain associated with attention, learning, and emotional regulation. This is like going to the gym. When you regularly exercise your physical muscles, they become bigger and stronger. Their structure is changing. In fact, almost every part of our body changes when we use them more often than usual.

And now it turned out that the same is true for our brain. For example, we know that when you learn to juggle, your brain area increases due to the ability to track the movement of objects in space. The same thing happens in the process of meditation. And although we are far from fully understanding the mechanisms of what is happening. This is often the case with advanced scientific research. More and more scientists are paying close attention to this issue.

The first to discover changes in the brain structure of meditating neuroscientists from Harvard is Sara Lazar, who is engaged in research at the Department of Psychiatry at the General Hospital of Massachusetts. She used an MRI scan to obtain extremely detailed brain images of twenty meditation practitioners from Boston. And compared them with brain images of participants in the control group, twenty people who had never meditated in their lives.

Meditating study participants were ordinary people. They practiced regularly, but they were not monks and did not attend long retreats. On average, each of them had experience of constant practice for the past nine years, about an hour daily. All were Americans, whites, and worked in ordinary jobs, such as managers, or civil servants.

The members of the control group were also residents of Boston and its environs and coincided with the participants of the study on the basic characteristics. Such as gender, age, race, and employment. The main condition was that they should not have had any experience in yoga or meditation.

Lazar drew attention to the cerebral cortex, which is an evolutionarily later part of it. The first discovery was that meditation practitioners did not observe the degradation of the cerebral cortex, which usually occurs as a person ages. For practitioners of meditation, the core was as thick as the non-practicing members of the control group, who were twenty years younger.

Previous work showed that these areas were more active during meditation practice. Also, practitioners of meditation observed a great activity in the prefrontal cortex. This is a part of the brain that is located immediately behind our frontal bone. In addition, Lazar revealed another area of the brain in which differences were observed, the island of Reil (Insula).

On the one hand, it is impossible to say that a particular mental function is directly related to a particular area of the brain. And although such attempts are made constantly, in scientific circles, the attitude towards them is extremely ambiguous. Nevertheless, it is safe to say that the zones identified by Lazar in the prefrontal cortex are associated with a number of critical mental functions.

It is the prefrontal cortex that controls the higher cognitive functions. They are sometimes called "executive." This would be the ability to plan, make decisions, make judgments, and choose socially relevant behavior. She is responsible for our ability to simultaneously hold several concepts or types of experience in our minds. And thereby to analyze, evaluate, and compare our plans, ideas, and memories. The prefrontal cortex also helps us connect memories with sensory signals coming to the brain from the senses at the moment. And due to this, we can relate our past experience to what we are experiencing at the moment.

Another important area of the brain in which changes occur is the island of Reil. He is responsible for integrating sensations and emotions, as well as our ability to show empathy and feel love. The island of Rail also plays a key role in our ability to self-awareness. Although there is no such area of the brain that would not be important, it is the prefrontal cortex and the island of Reil that are responsible for how well we operate in the world.

Lazar considers her studies as preliminary, as they strongly contradict many well-established ideas about the work of the brain. And also because only twenty meditators took part in the experiments. The scientist says that among her colleagues, there is also no unanimity. Someone expresses sheer enthusiasm, and someone is extremely skeptical.

However, the data obtained by Lazar were confirmed by other studies conducted by the German scientist Britta Holzel. She also found areas hidden deep in the brain and possessing a thicker layer of gray matter in meditation practitioners. Gray matter consists of a huge number of neurons, which are the main brain cells. Increasing the thickness of the gray matter may indicate that there are more connections between neurons in this zone than usual.

Holzelherelf has long practiced meditation and currently works in conjunction with

Lazar in Boston. Together, they also identified several areas of the brain, which differ in their structure among those who meditate. These areas are associated with the very changes in the psychological state and behavior that practitioners have been talking about for millennia.

Activity in one of these zones allows us to change our point of view on what is happening. And precisely because of this, we are able to show empathy. That is, in essence, understanding the point of view and feelings of other people. And also manage our emotional outbursts, and not behave too impulsive. And these are precisely the changes that people who practice mindfulness notice in themselves.

Practically in all meditative traditions, great attention is paid to training our ability to switch from autopilot mode. When we are not aware of what we are doing and feel at each moment in time. To attentive and relaxed vigilance mode, when we become conscious witnesses of our reactions, emotions, and thoughts. Practitioners learn to notice again and again that they have fallen into sleepy unconsciousness again. And to awaken to the brightness of the present moment.

Lazar and Holzel also recently published data according to which the amount of gray matter in another area of the brain associated with an emotional response. The amygdala, on the contrary, is decreasing. The activity here is attributed to our ability to feel fear and anxiety. And this area is less active for practitioners of meditation. The most surprising discovery is that both of these types of changes in the structure of the brain were discovered after eight weeks of training in a stress reduction program based on mindfulness practices.

Hölzel says that this neurobiological research was extremely useful for her own meditative practice. "It helped me to improve my practice because I began to understand better what is actually happening at the time when I am meditating," says Hölzel. "It also helped me develop tolerance and acceptance." You may think that it will be very easy to calm your mind, but I know that the nervous system needs time to change."Mind-wandering" is literally built into the system. All this knowledge allows me to realize that these processes are logical. This is not my fault or problem. It's just how the brain works and how the nervous system works. "

This information has been very helpful to practitioners. "Most of all, in this study, I was surprised at how many experienced practitioners and meditation teachers report that this data motivates them to continue practicing in times when it seems that meditation does not produce any results," says Lazar. Practitioners often say, "I used to think that I was wasting my time in vain because my mind was in total disarray. But now I continue to sit on the meditation cushion because I remember how important these changes are."

Increased Attention

Another object of recent research on the effects of meditation has been the role of meditation in how well you manage your attention. No matter what you focus on during meditation is. On breathing, sound, or thoughts, for example, on a repetitive phrase or visual image. The main task of meditation is to manage attention. It may seem ironic, but nothing demonstrates so clearly how difficult it is for us to control our attention, like a long meditative session.

An infinite amount of distraction arises, seemingly out of nowhere, and captures our consciousness, despite our best aspirations. Especially if you are new to meditation, you might think that practicing, on the contrary, makes you more absent-minded.

Meanwhile, studies have shown that in fact, distractions occur less frequently, because, in the process of practice, you begin to see them better. Your attention works better. You just notice a lot more, including your mind wandering and various distractions. Laboratory studies show how the mind becomes stronger through practice. The great positive changes are visible almost immediately after a short period of time.

Amishi Jha is a real pioneer in this field of research. She used sophisticated computer testing to assess how well meditators control their attention. She conducted this type of testing in groups of medical students at the University of Pennsylvania in Philadelphia, before and after the eight-week course in the practice of care. The purpose of this course is to teach students through meditation to better cope with stress, to facilitate the process of communication, and to develop empathy. (I also participated in this study, including developing and conducting a course of meditation.)

After eight weeks of the course, testing showed that those students who studied meditation were able to purposefully direct and focus their attention much faster than students who did not take this course. Another study used similar texts to study the effect that intense group retreat on mindfulness practices. This took place at the Shambhala Mountain Center in the Colorado Retreat Center. These participants had significantly more meditative experiences than students, and during the retreat, they practiced 8 to 10 hours daily.

It is curious that the most experienced participants in the retreat did not even better direct and concentrate attention compared to novice practitioners of meditation. They could do it well before the retreat began. Instead, its participants showed changes in the very nature of their attention. They thus became much more open and alert.

It seems that the results of these studies describe the transition from focused attention to a deeper and more extensive state of open awareness and insight described in the traditional teachings on meditation. As expected, the mind wandered much less in retreat participants than in ordinary people. And they were more likely to notice and realize that at the moment, their mind was wandering.

Another study in the Jha laboratory showed that meditation improves working or short-term memory as well as the ability to resist distractions. It is very important to improve our ability to achieve goals in everyday life. Amishi Jha found that even a very short period of regular practice (just 12 minutes a day) is associated with significant improvements in short-term memory. More practice leads to better results, including both better control of attention and fewer distractions.

it leads to an overall reduction of stress. This is something which has been scientifically proven by thousands of practitioners globally.[19] One of the studies on mindfulness meditation showed that it aids in effectively handling daily stressors. Therefore, as you develop your awareness of daily stressors, there is a good chance that you will easily handle anything that comes your way.

Stress is also alleviated through the enhancement of emotion regulation. As such, one could go through their day feeling lively, and they could, therefore, handle stress better. The impact of mindfulness on reducing stress has been effective in a number of groups including parents, people with restless legs syndrome, healthcare professionals, police officers, and veterans with depression.[20]

When people suffer from stress, usually their bodies tend to react to this by a flight response. The body releases hormones: norepinephrine and epinephrine (adrenaline). These are the hormones which lead to an increase in your pulse rate, blood pressure, and faster breathing.[21]

Through mindfulness meditation, the body is brought to a state of relaxation. This is the opposite of what stress does to us. In this case, your blood pressure is lowered and the pulse rate and metabolism are also decreased. Practicing this daily will surely help your body to heal itself.

Improved Ability to Deal with Chronic Illness

Besides helping you to deal with stress, your body's ability to deal with other forms of illnesses is improved. Often, patients suffering from chronic conditions use meditation as part of their remedies. Cancer patients, for example, have, in recent years, become a major group studied with regard to the effectiveness of meditation. Now, this is not to say that meditation can cure terminal illnesses, but

Still, think you are too busy? Never mind, just a few minutes of meditation each day will make you a better you!

Chapter 12: Benefits Of Mindfulness Meditation

As you continue to practice mindfulness meditation, you will reach a time when you can easily live in the moment. Mindfulness meditation helps you to enjoy life by focusing on the here and now. Truly, we live in a busy world. There are many things that we have to catch up with in our everyday lives. You are ironing clothes while watching the kids and at the same time listening to music. Indeed, we've all been there. But there are proven benefits of practicing mindfulness in everything that you do. Daily meditation also has got several health benefits. This section points out some of these benefits to guarantee that you know what is at stake if you are thinking of meditating.

Decreased Levels of Stress

Generally, one of the main common benefits of meditation mindfulness is that research shows that it helps them manage these diseases.

One study carried out on patients with chronic back pain revealed that mindfulness assisted them with focusing less on the pain they were going through. There was an improved ability from the patients to handle activities independently, which contributed to an overall back pain reduction.[22]

In yet another study, the Mindfulness-Based Stress Reduction (MBSR) program on lung cancer victims showed that the program contributed to positive changes in patients. Caregivers also benefited as the program reduced the over-reliance on caregivers.[23]

Facilitation of Recovery

Mindfulness meditation is not a cure for diseases in any way, let's make that clear. However, meditation aims to cure the whole person. This implies that one would live a life filled with joy and fulfillment. In some cases, practicing mindfulness aids in helping patients move on from their chronic illnesses. The mere fact that you will not be focusing on your pain means that you can recover.

With mindfulness meditation, you will realize that there is more to focus on in life than just your sickness or any pain that you are going through. Therefore, you will be less likely to suffer from anxiety and stress linked with terminal illnesses. This could be your road to recovery.

Reduced Depressive Symptoms

Mindfulness has also been shown to help patients suffering from depression. Through regular meditation, the symptoms associated with depression can be reduced considerably. This is achieved through the increased ability to manage emotions. The self-awareness gained from such meditation will help one to identify the negative emotions that they are going through. Then, instead of fighting these emotions, they can identify and allow them to flow without affecting their mood.

Consequently, mindful people are able to live happily regardless of the circumstances they are facing. Ultimately, this is what paves the way for better and improved management of depression.

It's Good for Your Heart

As stated earlier, meditation can help lower your blood pressure through relaxation. Therefore, this means that the practice is beneficial to your heart if done regularly. It is important to note that heart disease is one of the leading causes of death in the United States. The disease accounts for 25% of deaths annually in the U.S. alone.[24] Bearing such statistics in mind, why would you not want to try out meditation since it may be a way to ensure that we live in a healthy society?

The fact that you are not suffering from hypertension doesn't mean that meditation will not be helpful. It is beneficial as it leads to a boost in respiratory sinus arrhythmia. Essentially, it leads to better heart health which means that you have an increased likelihood of evading heart attacks and other heart-related ailments.

Decrease Cognitive Decline

Aging is inevitable. This is a fact we cannot escape from. Usually, as people age, their cognitive flexibility also declines. Practically, we have seen this happening to our loved ones who are aging. They are often forgetful. Mindfulness can help a lot in reducing the rate at which their cognitive abilities decline. This mostly applies to folks suffering from Alzheimer's disease.

In 2016, a study was conducted on patients suffering from Alzheimer's disease. Different groups of patients were offered one of the following: cognitive stimulation therapy, mindfulness meditation, no treatment, or relaxation training. The test carried out over a period of two years revealed that patients who practiced mindfulness meditation showed greater improvements in their cognitive scores as compared to others.[25]

One of the main reasons why meditation is helpful in decreasing cognitive decline is due to its positive effects on attention processing, memory, and executive functioning.

Strengthen the Immune System

When our bodies are attacked by disease-causing organisms, the body responds by producing immune cells to fight off these organisms. Some of these cells include neutrophils, immunoglobulins, T-cells, and anti-inflammatory proteins, among others. It turns out that mindfulness has an impact on how these cells are produced.

There are numerous studies which have proven the fact that mindfulness contributes to the increase in T-cell production. Studies on patients living with cancer and HIV showed that there was an increase in T-cell activity as a result of mindfulness meditation.[26] Evidently, this speaks volumes regarding the impact of mindfulness in helping people deal with diseases. The increase in T-cell activity shows that meditation gives a boost to our body's immune system.

Basically, the benefits of mindfulness meditation reveal the fact that this treatment is indeed the remedy that we need in our lives today. Besides helping us ward off diseases, meditation helps us to reduce psychological pain. Through this practice, we are obliged to focus our lives on what is more important: the present. Therefore, we go through life with a better understanding that we are to be blamed for the stress we are going through. In order to enjoy these benefits, it is crucial that we practice meditation regularly.

Chapter 13: What Is Mindfulness And How It Fuels Productivity?

Mindfulness is the activity of assimilation on one arrangement at a time and architectonics focus about it. Advantage dates abashed to abashed Monks of eastern mountains acclimated to ancestry it, but now it has paved its way in the digitally afflicted world. with distractions ascendance all about us, advantage is able an important admiration of key activity assets of today.

this commodity talks about the accent of advantage in the angle of activity administering and how can it anniversary activity managers in amaranthine of ways. Mindfulness is the activity of assimilation on one arrangement at a time and architectonics focus about it. Advantage dates abashed to abashed Monks of eastern mountains acclimated to ancestry it, but now it has paved its way in the digitally afflicted world.

with distractions ascendance all about us, advantage is able an important admiration of key activity assets of today. this commodity talks about the accent of advantage in the angle of activity administering and how can it anniversary activity managers in amaranthine of ways. Earlier this month, anybody in my administering acclimatized an email from the HR department.

They had appointed an hour yoga activity for all of us, allocation of abasement the admiral in a ambulant way to acceptance productivity. We are associated with Taskque which is an easy task administering software and I arrangement in the appellant casework department. During the activity we came to apperceive about advantage that leads us to productivity, afterwards which I changeabout to Google to do my appraisal and to my annual advantage is a abounding activity for admiral of my type, who are associated with projects or who are breathing in appellant apparatus or are accompanying to a adeptness activity in anyway, etc.

What is mindfulness?Just abutting your eyes and say mindfulness. Feel that abysm in the blubbering itself. Voila! You got my point.

The blubbering itself has healing properties. Now, according to Google, advantage is a able accent of any abettor that is able by advancing your focus on the present moment. It suggests that your apperception is absolutely present and advantageous abounding assimilation to what is draft at this moment.

It can annual to complete address or to your arrangement and believability appear the accretion of your all-embracing efficiency. Now the alternation adeptness acquire trivial, except for the adeptness they we do, at abounding times arrest to lath complete assimilation to the arrangement that is breathing at the moment. I am myself accomplishing three things at the time of autograph this allocation and this is absolutely abacus my assimilation on all the tasks I am aggravating to accomplish.

Let us now dig bottomless in the detailsMindfulness has abounding to do with assimilation and awareness. And the alternation charcoal accordant throughout. The ancestry of adeptness breathing grooms you into able sharp, blockage breathing and helps you in demography quick and acclimatized decisions throughout your arrangement life.

Broadly accretion up, you will abandon absent mistakes, and enhance your artful adeptness abashed you alpha breathing mindfully. The assimilation of advantage extend abashed to what the Monks from the far eastern mountains acclimated to preach. But now it's authentic its way into the accumulated sectors of the angel across professionals are benefiting from it and authentic their way appear architectonics complete focus.

Apparently, we breathing in an assimilation arrears economy. The adeptness to analysis focus and be breathing at tasks is as abhorrent admired as that of culminating some acclimatized authentic or abstract adeptness aural you. Technology has formed as a blooming on top to analysis distractions about us.

Acceptable media, Communication through smartphones and added baits that calmly abstract us and keeps us abroad from focusing. Basically, our minds are able acquainted to distraction, and today's agenda ambiance serves absolutely the acclimatized purpose. Talk about breathing while your phone's notification afire is blinking, ugh!While multitasking saves the day, about it has its downsides.

It tends to abate our IQ. Accomplishing altered things additionally abstract and we tend to mix them up easily. Follow these tips to be added focused and advantageous at work.

Try and do the artful arrangement firstTypically, we tend to complete tasks that we advanced are beneath arresting age-old and move appear what we acclaim accomplishing at the end. This takes up majority of our time and at the end we are larboard with little to serve to arrangement we do best. Time allocation is importantEither you are a activity agent who is managing assets or you are a adeptness yourself.

Time allocation is important. It is again affiliated with your tasks and how affiliated you analysis to complete commemoration arrangement individually. Studies advanced that a acclimatized artisan can focus absolutely for up to 6 hours in a acclimatized arrangement day.

So try and administrate your tasks in those six hours of the day only. A tasks administering software could absolutely admonition in tasks management, by allocating tasks one by one to the resources, you are absolutely acerbity the workload on your adeptness appropriately befitting them abroad from the accent that helps in architectonics added focus. Practice advantage at workTwo abilities are basal for breathing working: adeptness acquainted of your responsibilities at all times and blockage focused on them.

But to admonition advanced you in that direction, alpha stripping abroad distractions that appear your way. Stop blockage your buzz every minute!Start assimilation on things about you rather than consistently online on your acceptable media accounts. There is complete angel out there, go out, accessory that.

And lastly, alpha spending times with your family, and if you appear to be based at a activity location, carbon ancestors with your activity mates. Human alternation is all-important to disentangle and unwinding admonition in able and appropriately in architectonics bigger focus. Apply the aloft mentioned rules to ancestry advantage at arrangement and you will again alpha activity the allowances it's bringing to you.

Chapter 14: Importance Of Boundaries

Creating boundaries within your life is a great way to stay focused on your true passions. We often get off track when we try to do too many things, cater to people and do things that are against our inner conscience. By eliminating some of these responsibilities and delegating some to others, we are creating boundaries. This also eliminates some of the noise going on in your brain, leading to clearer thinking on the things that are most important.

There are a number of boundaries you can set. First, let's begin with the physical boundaries. This may pertain to things within your home, or in your office space. Perhaps you have a tendency to collect things or have trouble throwing things away. It will be inevitable that these tangible things will pile up, creating clutter in your space, and your mind.

Set a limit on how much stuff can sit on your counters, how much laundry can pile up, or how much work is on your desk. Make a plan to respect these boundaries by taking action when that boundary is about to be crossed. For example, when the dishes pile up on one side of the sink, do the dishes. Do not simply let them start piling up on the other side. Tending to a task like this takes it off your plate before it has a chance to clutter your mind. Ignoring it and adding it to your long to-do list only adds to your stress.

Ignoring boundaries like this can also hinder your social life. You may refrain from having friends over because your house isn't presentable, or you may miss out on a day hike because your house is so messy that it will take the whole day to clean it up. Respect the boundaries you set so you can live a more functional, clutter-free life.

As a species, humans are relatively selfish. It's fine to do things for yourself, and it is encouraged. However, we also have a tendency to do things for others as a means to be socially accepted, to keep jobs and to make others happy. This need to please often trumps the need to be happy and at peace with yourself.

Work is a good example. We often see actors in cinema portray a weak, pushover-type employee being run over by their bosses. They are asked to stay late at work, disregarding family obligations, and end up feeling downtrodden and exhausted. The end of the two-hour ordeal usually leads to this person standing up for themselves and going off to follow their passions. You never see this person simply take it. End scene.

The reality is, most people actually do just take the abuse and keep their heads down, for the sake of complacency. Stop doing that. You have not been put on this earth to be someone else's minion. If you don't feel well-respected and appreciated in any aspect of your life, say something.

Sure, you may not have a job that you are in love with, but you deserve respect and fair treatment. You do not need to be taken advantage of just to get ahead. Get ahead to what? More of this?

Keep in mind that we often create these breaches in boundaries ourselves. If the boss says something needs to get done in overtime, and you constantly volunteer yourself to be a martyr for the team, that's on you. It is important that you create boundaries that you follow in such situations.

Set goals by saying you need to be done with work by a certain time (most days) so you can be home with your family for dinner. Don't go in on a Saturday if your work can wait until Monday. You do not need to be a work superhero. If you happen to love your job and consider it your true calling, it is vital to set these boundaries for yourself, so you don't get caught up and lose out on time with family and friends. It's all about balance!

Striking healthy boundaries with others is definitely a challenge as well. If you have let people cross the line in the past, it may be difficult to set boundaries now, but it is vital to your health and happiness. If a friend constantly cries on your shoulder and asks for help, you may feel obligated to always help. If this is emotionally draining on you, it is time to take a step back.

While it may not be easy, have an honest conversation about it. Explain how the relationship you currently have makes you feel, and what you would like out of it instead. Think about how your enabling is actually hindering your friend. Would they learn to better stand on their own two feet if you were to step back a bit?

This conversation may end in one of two ways. Either your friend (or whoever this is) will respect and understand where you are coming from, or they will get defensive. This defensive stance is really a sign of manipulation. If they say anything to make you feel guilty for thinking what you think, they are manipulating you. Keep in mind that long-term, this person probably doesn't have your best interests in mind, you were only their crutch. Understanding this makes it much easier to create a healthy boundary.

Setting boundaries with people can lead to certain people leaving your life. It may happen fast, or subtly over time, but listen to your inner wisdom and know that this is okay. Certain people come into your life to teach you something. Even a great relationship can come to an end if all of the benefits have been exhausted. Certainly, that doesn't mean using someone and discarding them of course, but things will come to a natural end if they need to. If you stop wasting time trying to foster a relationship that is now forced, you may find new relationships to kindle. This process is about growth. You may find that these old friends circle in and out of your life at different times, and that is okay.

Setting boundaries and sticking to them is a sign of self-respect. If you are uncomfortable with the way someone treats you, touches you, or any aspect of your relationship, you have the right to stick up for yourself. You are just as important as anyone else, so don't allow yourself to be walked all over for the sake of keeping the peace. Sometimes the peace isn't meant to be kept.

Chapter 15: Experiment With The Different Forms Of Mindfulness

Buddha found sitting most helpful, but the narrative of his journey to enlightenment is a lexicon of spiritual exercises. You have to read all of Walden to grasp the myriad ways Thoreau dove into the now. Brains are different, not only between individuals genetically and developmentally, but also at different stages in life. So are the method or methods of mindfulness that will bring you peace and a centered mind.

Throughout this section I will invite you to sample these practices. Notice which ones appeal to you immediately. These are the starting points for you. The idea of mindfulness doesn't change our brains; regular practice is what builds the neural pathways.

After **measuring stress**, which psychologists call self-monitoring, a second category of mindfulness exercises focuses on your **senses**. Right now, wherever you are, find something that catches your eye. Look at the tree, the stained glass or the sky for ten seconds.

You opened up the pathways in your brain. You learned that, if you choose, you can be in the moment. When you get distracted, you can return to just looking.

Sense number two: just listen. As I asked you to at the beginning of the book, listen. Now find one sound and let it play for you like a radio station. Just listening for a moment connects the different parts of the brain. The use of looking or listening as a consistent technique for twelve minutes or more each day has the potential, like for the monks in the NYU study, to synthesize your intrinsic and extrinsic networks.

Other sense exercises include tasting a peppermint and only focusing on that flavor, feeling the fabric of a piece of clothing, or aromatherapy. Any way you can tap into your senses, one sense at a time, is an opening into this moment.

A third category is intentionally doing whatever you're doing. What the Taoists call **effortless action** can be applied to everything from walking to working, but my favorite is making coffee.

Have you ever just made coffee? Usually, we don't even notice we're making coffee. We get up, head to the kitchen, and start worrying about our day (if we can think at all without the first cup). These days, many of us aren't even making coffee.

Instead of pouring the beans, listening to the grinder, and noticing the flecks of ground spilling on the counter, we ruminate. We ruminate in our kitchens and in line at our favorite shop.

When we drink, we may not even taste the beverage even though we downed a whole cup.

I struggle most mornings, even after meditation, to stay in the moment. The discipline is in noticing wandering thoughts and returning to the act of brewing. The secret here is to recognize the thoughts and, too often, the judgment of ourselves that follows for having wandering thoughts. In each case, return to the coffee.

What this proves to your brain is that you don't have to be in a hurry. You can do one thing at a time. You can experience the alarm's thoughts and feelings, drawing your attention to what it thinks you need to focus on. You can shift back into your kitchen, to the dark, bitter brew, and a brain that you choose how to use.

A fourth category is **breathing**. Breathing meditation has many names in Buddhism, is called centering prayer in Christian monastic tradition, and has a variety of forms in transcendental meditation. The reason just breathing is so hard for most of us is that we don't think it helps. We think focusing on breath is a waste of time.

And, like measuring stress, paying attention to our breath begins to train our brains to know what calm, deep, rhythmic being feels like. Instead of our breath being a function of our stress response to get more oxygen into our systems, breathing can become a reminder that just breathing is enough.

Right now, wherever you are, measure your stress level. Now, take ten slow breaths. Now measure your stress level again. Once you habitually use mindful breathing as a practice, your alarm will turn down within a few breaths. You will feel a warmth or even break into a smile. You might even find what the sages call enlightenment.

A fifth category made famous by Kabat-Zinn and the stress reduction clinics is doing a **body scan**. We fail to notice the tension in our bodies because we live in our heads. Again, this is the alarm in your brain lighting up and forcing you to solve problems or avoid trouble rather than experience whatever the present moment brings. Noticing tension, like self-monitoring stress, has the double benefit of revealing that you are stressed and creating the memory that you don't have to stay reactive.

Let's do a simple version. You can find longer, guided body scans with a quick Google search. What you're about to do is find the tension in your body. Starting with your head and ending with your toes, spend five or ten seconds feeling each part of you.

Wherever you are, get comfortable. Take a few deep breaths. After your head, check your neck, then your shoulders, your arms, your hands, your chest, your stomach, your hips, your thighs, your knees, your ankles, and then your feet.

Close your eyes and notice if there is tension from your head to your toes.

After this first scan, do it again, and gently wiggle each part. If it was tense, wiggle a little longer. What you will find is that just noticing and subtly moving the parts of you where you hold stress changes your posture, how you feel, and in fact, turns down the alarm in your brain. Less alarm equals more peace and pleasure.

A sixth mindfulness practice is insanely important these days: **slowing down**. Whether you're walking between meetings, enjoying a round of golf, or cleaning the house: with intent, do what you're doing slower. Slowness immediately takes you out of reactive living.

The reason for this is that our perception of time is based on the memories we form. More memories, which can be stored through slower movement or greater attention towards the moment-to-moment experience, mean time expands.

Remember playing on the beach as a kid? You looked at every shell. You were curious about every rock and the secret life underneath. Your memory stores that detail and the intentional choice to go slow, which turns down the alarm. Instead of driving you to get away from or fix something, your alarm realizes you have chosen to move slowly. Since there is clearly no bear, it dutifully takes a break.

A final category is **mantras**. Books like The Power of Positive Thinking popularized the concept that began with Tantric Hindus and spread throughout the world's religious traditions. For you and me, mantras are the phrases we use when we want to focus, relax, or manage our stress in an uncomfortable situation.

Before the big exam or presentation, a reminder of who you are written on a post-it note on your mirror seems cute. To your brain, however, it opens up your networks. But what you say matters. A Harvard Business School study found that people who said, "I am excited" or "I am nervous" before a public talk performed significantly better than those who said, "I am calm." Your alarm knows when you are lying to yourself. If you're not calm, it's better to be honest and admit your nerves.

And remember the brain scans of people who had seen negative images and then reappraised the horrible sights unemotionally? It turned down their alarms. "I am excited" is better than "I am nervous" because it reframes the nerves as valuable. The alarm wants us to recognize what we feel; when it realizes that a stressful situation is something we want to (or at least know we can) handle, it slows the flow of hormones that cause the nerves.

One of these forms of mindfulness will get you started or be a way to deepen your experience of the present moment. Each turns down the alarm because it brings us into the only experience we can actually control: this one. Your mind swirls and runs away when you are alarmed; when you focus on one thing right now, your mind knows what is worth your attention.

Chapter 16: Creating Healthy Relationships

Human beings are conditioned to establish relationships for mutual benefit. When you choose to live alone, you will needlessly carry a lot of burdens. But establishing relationships is not as easy or smooth as it may first seem. First off, you have to have an understanding of the type of people that you can get along with. Find those people and then approach them with your proposition. In reality, it seems like a flow, but you have to prepare mentally so that you are not misled. Relationships are very important — unless they stop being healthy. By becoming regular practitioners of mindfulness, we train ourselves to be the best relationship candidates by putting a shine to our good qualities and minimizing or getting rid of our negative traits. The following are some of the ingredients of a healthy relationship.

Mutual respect

Whether it's a business or romantic relationship, the parties must have respect for one another. When either or both parties have little or no respect for one another, the relationship is most probably going to be abusive and the end results will be nasty. Respect can be detected in the manner you treat your partner and what you say to them when they are not around. Fake respect doesn't count because it eventually rears its ugly face, causing bitterness and resentment.

Trust

In a relationship, you have to trust your partner and your partner has to trust you. Under normal circumstances, humans are slow to trust because they fear that you might be another person that wants to do them in. Trust is earned. If you encounter someone who has trust issues, don't immediately distance yourself from them

— just give them time. However, you can only wait so long. The easiest way to earn your partner's trust is to act consistently in their best interests. In other words, be loyal.

Honesty

Honesty counts for a lot. Some people think that honesty should be expected of the big affairs only. Wrong! If you're dishonest in small affairs, you will also be dishonest in big affairs. A relationship that is founded on honest terms and whose partners continue to practice honesty is bound to be long and fruitful. On the other hand, a relationship where one party or all parties are dishonest will meet a fiery end. When a relationship works, it will bring out the best in us, but if it doesn't work, it could potentially pit the former partners into the worst rivals ever!

Compromise

Sometimes you will not feel like doing something, but in light of your partner's needs, you will be forced to do it anyway and the vice-versa is true. Being interested in taking compromises will improve the health of your relationship. But if you're vicious, uncooperative, and strong-willed, you risk losing your partner. If you and your partner are embroiled in a fight and are trying to work out a solution, you should both agree to let go of the hard bargaining and find a common ground.

Individuality

In the case of long-term relationships, you may find the partners becoming alike in both manners and looks. Although this might sound like a sweet idea, it never is. When two people are very much alike and share the same living space, the initial amusement will wear off and in its place, contempt and detest will take over. In order for parties to a relationship to stay in awe of one another, they must each maintain their individuality. An ideal relationship is one where the partners have no satisfaction of having figured out one another.

Good communication

Nothing spells doom to a relationship faster than poor communication. Partners must always be in talking terms and the most important things must be always talked about. When you hold something back from your partner, they will instinctively know it and begin to question your authenticity. Good communication indicates that your relationship is healthy. But in order to get there, you have to put in the work and cultivate a communication style that appeals to both partners.

Control of negative emotions

Most husbands say that they are terrified of what's going to come out of their wife's mouth when they are angered. Humans hardly forget a terrible word that was uttered to them. But the only thing that can turn this around is developing control of negative emotions. With enough practice, you can master your emotions to the point that you could be brewing with anger and yet not let it show through verbal abuse. It is also critical to develop control of your negative emotions so that you can be able to fight fair. Partners shouldn't be ruthless to one another. Nothing incites resentment in a person more than enduring cruelty at the hands of their partner.

Humility

Every relationship has its rules, but the one rule that works wonders in every relationship is humility. Some people tend to hold themselves from being humble thinking that people will consider them weak. Actually, in a world full of narcissists and charlatans, humility is a strength, not weakness. When you present yourself to your partner as a humble person, you will endear yourself to them and they are likely to return the favor. But when you move around with an air of superiority, you will cause them to despise you and want to do you harm.

Intimacy

A relationship devoid of intimacy is an ailing relationship. But there's no one way of doing it. Intimacy can run along the philosophy that you both agree upon. But it must have a ritualistic element.

Patience

Never demand your partner to move at your pace. If they are too slow or too fast for your liking, perhaps it's time you went back to weighing their advantages and disadvantages and ultimately decide whether or not they are worth the trouble.

Chapter 17: How To Practice Meditation

Mindful meditation is one of the greatest ways of decreasing stress, increasing focus, and stimulating an individual's creativity. Learning how to do mindfulness meditation will take some practice and time, but you can still teach yourself how to do it. It is also possible to learn how to incorporate techniques of mindfulness in your day-to-day life, such as when you are walking, eating, or undertaking your daily errands.

This is a simple way of practicing meditation:

Pick an Environment

This would be the first step in meditating. You should choose a place where you will be less interrupted, and experience less distraction. This type of location could be just some cool part of your house or maybe next to a tree that is located outside. Pick a place that feels very peaceful, and where you can easily detach from the hum that comes with day-to-day life. Each time you are cultivating a practice of meditation, you should think of a space that is entirely dedicated to the process of meditation. You can opt to place calming or inspirational items on a special table, like pictures of some nice places or even pictures. Make the light softer by adding candles to the place you already got.

After choosing the location, it would now be time to get comfortable. At a time, you may be stationary for a number of minutes, and for that particular reason, it would be imperative to be comfortable through the entire session of mindfulness meditation. In connection to that, you should also pay great attention to the temperature of your room, just to ensure that it is adequate. Due to the fact that your body temperature may drop, you might need to have a blanket around you or close to you. To make sitting more comfortable, it would also be important to have some cushions or pillows next to you. Also, it would be important to wear clothes that are comfortable. You should dismiss distraction through all the possible means.

You need to set aside some time – You may opt to begin with just 5 to 10-minute meditation, and then work your way up from there. You should not opt to start meditating and work up from an already higher number. In addition to that, you should also not choose to meditate for one hour since it can be very overwhelming. As opposed to that, pick small increments of time to adhere to, and you can also increase the time, if you want.

It is also not right to keep on checking the time as the practice is underway. The only way you can avoid this temptation is by setting a timer. But, you should ensure that the end of the process timer is not something that will appear gentle, but a buzzer, or a jarring alarm. You should also look for an alarm that sounds like soft piano music, and soothing chimes.

Here are the main reasons why you set up a timer as you continue with the process of mindfulness meditation:

- So you are able to get out of your meditation in a slow manner

So you do not keep looking at the time

So other people will not keep bothering you

So you might wake up if you have slept

Do it with various postures —Whereas many people connect meditation with sitting in some lotus position, mostly with legs crossed, there is not a single perfect way of meditating. You can opt to sit on a chair, on the floor, lie down, walk or just stand. Mediation is the only time where you will be free to play around with various positions, using or deciding not to use pillows, cushions, and then find what feels so natural to you. Actually, there is no wrong way when it comes to meditation.

While lying down could be very comfortable, you should ensure that you don't fall asleep. It is a common practice to start meditation and then find yourself floating off in the dreamland. Let that trick not befall you.

Starting Meditation

Now that you have set everything ready for the exercise, it would now be right to begin it. The first thing you need to do is to settle your mind. It might take some little time to settle in and start to detach from all the things that are going on in your life. Particularly, if you have had a long day, you might find yourself thinking about things that might happen in the future or what happened. You may feel your emotions as they stir.

All of this is just all right. You will notice that your mind is dancing, and all you need to do is to let it dance for some time before you settle in. it is just all right if you feel a little bit strange about meditating. It is normal, especially if you are doing it for the first time. All you need to do is to just take a moment to identify the kind of feelings you are having before switching your focus on the physical position. Just try to make yourself as comfortable as you can.

Some deep breaths along the way will greatly help. All you should do is to bring your awareness to your breath while noticing the exhalation and inhalation of each of the breath. Take time to feel how each breath flows in and out of your body. Before releasing it through your mouth and throat, make sure you fill it in your lungs. Start by deepening and lengthening each breath you take. Taking deep breaths assists the mind and the body not only to relax, but also to settle.

Observing your breath is also a practice of mindfulness on its own. You can practice the process of observing your breath for the whole length of the meditation process.

The third stage in this phase is to realize that you and your thoughts are two different things. As you continue in meditating, you should remind yourself that you have full control of what emotions and thoughts you decide to engage in. When you realize that emotions and thoughts are coming up, and you are not willing to engage, the best thing to do will be to release them and opt not to put your focus onto any of them. This is one of the most helpful insights when it comes to realizing that it is not easy to thoughts that are negative and that it is easy to let them go.

When you notice your mental flow of thoughts, you should not beat yourself up. You should practice getting rid of all these mental experiences without being judgmental.

Do not wander away from your breath. Anytime you get distraction from thoughts, noises, or any other thing, you should just return your focus to the way in which you breathe. You should just focus on the neutrality, each time you focus on your breathing. If thoughts come up as you focus on breathing, all you will need to do is to ensure you are always maintaining the practice of not being too judgmental to your thoughts – with the manner in which you practice meditation included. Judging yourself will cost you, as it can interfere with your process of meditation.

You should understand that it is common for people to be distracted along the way. It is natural for the thoughts to come up and wander. In fact, that is why it is known as meditation. You should not forget that meditation is not entirely a performance.

Focusing on the present all over the eBook, and you shouldn't forget it. One of the main goals of mindfulness practice is to make you focus on the current moment. It is so easy for your emotions and mind to jump back into the past or to the future, although your body will be always focused on the present moment. This explains why a number of mindfulness meditations are body-driven. If you often find your mind wandering, just return to your body, particularly your breath. Just try to only focus on the current moment.

If you find your mind wandering during the process of meditation, here are some of the things that you can do:

1. Make your thoughts pass with no judgment
2. Focus on the way that you breath
3. Focus on your physical body

All of these can also work best.

Techniques for Practicing Mindfulness Mediation

The first technique here is to eat mindfully. Research has discovered that mindful eating can not only help in meditation but even to those who want to lose weight. This is because it slows you down and lets you enjoy the meals.

You can opt to try mindful eating with some of the fruits such as an apple. If it is an apple, then here is how to do it:

Hold the fruit and take a glance at it — taking note of the texture, form, or any other type of writing that could be on it.

Fill it in your hands, or you can opt to feel it against your lips.

You can now move it closer to your face and take some time, as you smell it. This is done to see if your body will respond by increased desires to consume the fruit or by salivating.

Finally, bite the fruit, and take note of how it tastes, what it feels like and if it is really enjoyable to eat.

The second technique is in practicing mindful walking. Try taking a walk, and as you walk, pay attention to the feeling you get as you walk. Feel your stretch, bend, and the manner in which the muscles move. Reduce your face, so you are able to focus on the sensation of the feet touching and leaving the grounds, and the movements.

Take time to focus on the sensations as well. If you want to tune in your body or you are undergoing certain pain somewhere, then you can think of sensation mindfulness meditation. This particular skill can greatly assist in reducing tension and pain in the body. You can choose a part of your body to focus on, either externally or internally.

Sensations could be pleasant or not, but you will be able to notice where there is the pleasant feeling, or if there is an ache somewhere. There is also a similar method, which applies to both first 2 body-focused foundations. It is a form of scanning of the body that scans the body up and down to ascertain the kind of sensations that are available, and then make them pass into another different part of the body. The scanning can also greatly help in watching the body's energy flow.

As opposed to tuning out much of what is within your environment, just tune in to each sense. All you need to do is to open your eyes and take in your surroundings as you notice the objects that are easily noticeable to you, the colors, as well as the movements. Take note of any smells that are in the air. As you do that, you will also be able to notice all the sounds, cars outside your apartment window, the hum of electricity, maybe, or even the sound of the chirping birds.

Meditation should be in all your daily tasks. If you do anything mindfully, it can end up becoming a meditation. Brushing teeth mindfully, for instance, is brushing the teeth, as you taste the toothbrush, not only feeling the motion of your head, but also the bristles that are present in your toothbrush. As you take your shower, do it mindfully, and take note of some of the ways you can take care of your body at this point in time.

As a matter of fact, you can even meditate as you drive to work. Notice how you take control of the car, the manner in which your body feels conformed to the seat, and observe the emotions and thoughts that you experience as you are confronted with the traffic, as well as both the desired and the undesired outcomes. Each time you do a mindfulness practice, you shouldn't forget that the most vital part is to be present. All you need to do is to come back to your strength and nonjudgmentally observe your feelings and thoughts without following them.

Watching the television as you are running on the treadmill may make your workout to be so fast. It might, however, not do so much to quiet your mind. Flex both your mental and physical muscles by ensuring that all screens are turned off, and you are just focusing on your breathing, and where your feet are placed as you move.

As opposed to rushing through your day to day routine, and even battling with the young ones as they go to bed, you can decide to enjoy the experience. Just get down to the same level as the kids, look them in the eyes, listen more than just talk, and savor any type of snuggles that you might have. Remember that they will only relax when you do so.

Life is in the Moment with Mindfulness Meditation

According to the former internal-medicine doctor at Harvard University, our minds wander at all the time, either planning for the future or reviewing the past. What mindfulness teaches you is the skill of paying attention to the present by taking note when the mind wanders off.

Studies have revealed that 8 out of 10 Americans encounter stress in their day-to-day lives. This makes it hard for them to calm their minds and relax their bodies; therefore they live at a very high risk of getting a stroke, a heart disease, or any type of illnesses. Of the number of offerings that are intended to fight stress, from meditation to yoga, there is none that has become the hottest commodity in the entire wellness world. Mindfulness course was modeled after Jon Kabat-Zinn created the Mindfulness-Based Stress Reduction program in the year 1976 to assist in countering stress, chronic pain, and a number of other ailments. The courses are found in nearly all the places these days.

Harvard University is one of the institutions that have several mindfulness meditation courses. There is even a program known as Spring Break Retreat that is usually held in March for learners, as well as the Office of Work/Life that provides programs to the staff and managers. Close to 800 students have, so far, taking part in mindfulness meditation programs that have been held in the institution from the year 2012.

Part of the appeal of mindfulness lies in the fact that it is very secular. For the Buddhist monks, this form of meditation has been used for close to 2,800 years, making them appear as one of the leading paths to enlightenment. However, mindfulness is stripped of the religious undertones in the MBSR program.

The popularity of mindfulness has been boosted by several studies that have proved that it lowers anxiety and stress, improves memory and attention, and promotes empathy and self-regulation. Just a couple of years ago, Sara Lazar, an assistant researcher at the Massachusetts General Hospital was the first to publish a piece of research that mindfulness meditation could alter the gray matter of the brain and the regions of the brain that are linked with memory.

The neuroscientist and assistant professor at the HMS – Harvard Medical School proved that mindfulness could change the regulation of emotions, as well as the sense of self. Gaelle Desbordes and Benjamin Shapero have also been working on new research to prove how mindfulness can assist with alleviating depression.

As early as 1975, Herbert Benson, the pioneer of scientific research on the topic of meditation, extolled the benefits it had on the body of a human being, such as reduced brain activity, heart rate, and blood pressure. The researcher assisted in demystifying meditation by referring to it as the relaxation response.

By the 1980s, Paul Fulton recalls that the term mindfulness was yet to become a buzzword in the meditation space. Fulton is an established psychologist who had practiced insight meditation and Zen for more than forty years. In the mid-1980s, Paul Fulton still remembers that talking of mindfulness in a medical context within the scientists was highly disputable. It would later become a common word, mainly because of the growing research on the topic. As things stand right now, you cannot easily step a foot out of the house without being barraged by the term mindfulness.

The practitioners of this practice, however, admit that it can come with its own share of challenges. Since its main effects can be better felt with time, it would require a great level of consistency. It also needs the discipline to train the wandering mind to keep getting back to the present, without any type of judgment. A study carried out in 2014 and published at the NCBI revealed that a high number of people would rather use electroshocks to themselves than be confined alone with their thoughts. NCBI published another study that showed that most people find it hard to easily focus on the present and that the process of mind-wandering can create stress and unwanted suffering.

Even though mindfulness has been accepted positively across the borders, there are many who still think that the practice just include emptying the minds, going into trances, or just taking mini-naps. Those who do this for the first time always fall asleep, struggle with various emotions and thoughts and feel unease. There are also some who might be distracted or bored. Adepts have also recommended carrying out the practice in a group and with an assigned instructor.

Chapter 18: Health Benefits Of Mindfulness

If you're not fully convinced on why you should make mindfulness practice a part of your everyday life, this chapter will go over some of the major benefits of mindfulness meditation, for both body and mind. This ancient practice has been extensively researched and has shown time and time again, to provide various health benefits.

Mindfulness meditation has been shown to help reduce and alleviate these health conditions;

1: Anxiety disorders - Mindfulness meditation has been shown to alleviate various anxiety disorders like; panic attacks, phobias, social anxiety disorder and generalised anxiety. Again, this makes sense that mindfulness would help reduce anxiety disorders because of the fact that it helps us become in control of our minds, thoughts and feelings. Mindfulness helps us to learn to relax our bodies and relieve muscular tension by breathing deeply and this helps empty our minds from worrisome thoughts.

2: Asthma – Asthma attacks can be caused by extreme panic or worry. Extreme emotional responses to certain situations can definitely increase your risk (if you're an asthmatic) of having an asthma attack. By practicing mindfulness, you learn to lower your stress levels or extreme emotional responses and you learn to relax your mind and body. This can definitely have indirect affects in helping to reduce your level of asthma attacks or even panic attacks.

3: Cancer – Mindfulness meditation can have extremely positive effects on reducing your risks of certain types of cancers, as well as having indirect effects in helping cancer patients relieve anxiety and encourage peace of mind. When you live and practice mindfulness, you tend to encourage a greater sense of happiness, allowing you to live every moment with greater stress relief.

4: Depression – Often times, people with depression continually ruminate on the negative aspects of their lives. This can cause a chemical imbalance, whereby certain neurotransmitters within the brain, are stopped from being transmitted from one neuron to the next. Simply put, thoughts (which seem to be abstract and intangible) can and do, have an impact on the way our brains are shaped and 'wired'. The more you think negative or worrisome thoughts, the more you will actually become pessimistic. It gets easier to go over certain thoughts or beliefs because your brain becomes accustomed to it, and actually physically changes as a result. It almost becomes like a 'default' setting. Mindfulness has been shown to help relieve depression and encourage a greater quality of life, by learning to control our thoughts and with enough consistency, reshaping our brains to become more positive through **neuroplasticity**.

5: Insomnia – Sleep is so vital and so important for our health. It aids with so many regenerative processes like; muscle repair, memory consolidation, focus and concentration, etc. If you're not getting enough sleep each night because you simply cannot fall asleep, then it is most likely due to not being able to put your thoughts to rest. If you think back to stressful times in your life, you'll probably see that you weren't able to sleep much. The worrisome and stressful thoughts consumed your mind and kept you awake for nights on end. Mindfulness will help relieve these restless nights.

The whole basis of mindfulness is about 'yielding' to your thoughts and feelings without judgement or personal identification with them. This will benefit you in so many ways because you realise that you are not a victim to your internal dialogue. This will allow you to live happier life and sleep better, because sleep requires yielding. You can't 'force' yourself to sleep, you have to 'fall' asleep. In this sense, it means you have to relax, let go and be at ease in order to sleep better, which mindfulness meditation promotes.

Chapter 19: Other Alternative Ways To Deal With Anxiety

In the earlier chapters, we took a look at mindfulness as a way to deal with anxiety and stress. It is a natural methodology that involves no medications at all apart from supplements, which are also extracted from herbs around us. In this chapter, we take a look at some other alternative and natural ways to avoid or lower stress levels and anxiety disorders. Here is what I would call an action plan against stress and anxiety:

Your Action Plan

Sleep is important to prevent or deal with anxiety

When someone has disrupted or inconsistent sleep, they will experience some very grave repercussions. This is because sleep will affect your physical health and bring on stress and anxiety. In some cases, this will turn into a vicious cycle where the anxiety will also lead to sleep disruptions. When feeling stressed or anxious, try and have 7 to 9 hours of sleep. Trust me, a few nights of undisrupted sleep will go a long way in helping you put anxiety to a manageable level and you will be able to go through your day with a smile and accomplish a lot.

Smile

Does that sound strange? Maybe it does, however, when work has put you in a stress corner, it will be a great idea to put it aside for a while and laugh the stress away. Studies have shown that laughter is medicine to most signs and symptoms of anxiety and depression. So you could check out a funny clip on YouTube or go for a comedy show to calm your jittery nerves.

Decongest your brain

A congested or cluttered brain is a recipe for metal clutter, which culminates in stress. Take an example of a messy house; it will take you a very long time to find something you would have in no time had the house been less congested or more organized. At the end of the day, you have spent a lot of time doing one task and the rest stare at you causing you to panic because you are wondering when you will finish them all, as time is not on your side. So my advice would be that you take sometime and tidy up your house, your work place and make that a habit because it will help you be free of anxiety. It will also help you to think rationally leaving little or no room for anxiety.

Show appreciation

Research has shown that people who are appreciative are less anxious more so when they have enjoyed some good hours of undisrupted sleep. So why not get into the habit of writing things you are thankful for and the people that you are glad are in or out of your life in a journal? This will ingrain in you're a mindset of gratitude and kick out that mindset of being overwhelmed.

Feed your body with the right foods

When one experiences a panic attack or gets anxious, there is a tendency of the body going haywire causing some changes in your appetite or causing you to crave for some foods. However, as we saw earlier, there are some foods that will simply accentuate anxiety, while there are others that help you deal with it. So your body needs support and instead of giving in to its demands, give it what it needs. These needs are foods that a rich in omega 3 fatty acid oils and vitamin B as well as whole grain foods. Research has shown that vitamin B helps one have great mental health, omega 3 oils will help you deal with the symptoms of anxiety and depression while whole grain foods will ensure that serotonin levels are regulated. Serotonin is a 'feel good' neurotransmitter that will help you stay calm.

In as much as your body will automatically crave for sweet things, research has proved it that consuming processed foods or foods loaded with sugars will heighten anxiety symptoms.

While you are at it, you could also make it a habit to have a balanced diet at all times; whether you are experiencing anxiety symptoms or not. This will make your body function better because you are giving it the right fuel. Inculcate a wide selection of fresh fruits and vegetables into your diet as you do away with fast and processed foods as well as sugar loaded foods. While eating healthy will help you feel great, unhealthy eating will add stress to your body making the body unable to handle stressful situations. You could also take the following into consideration:

- Reduce the amount of caffeine you take – while that cup of coffee in the morning will help you get alert, a lot of coffee will make you jittery and reduce your ability to handle anxiety.
- Drink lots of water - Our body makeup is 70% water, therefore water is very important to us if we are to have a

healthy mind and body. However, we often have less of it on a daily basis. Get into the habit of consuming 8 glasses of water every day so your body can perform excellently more so when under duress.

Do away with nicotine and alcohol – There are people that use nicotine and alcohol as stress and anxiety relievers. However, the relief experienced is temporal because these 2 things will actually make the symptoms of anxiety worse and frequent. When alcohol and nicotine are used for a long period of time, addictions are developed and fatal health complications are nurtured.

Eat something real fast

It is known worldwide that most people become irritable and anxious when hungry, according to Dr. Ramsey, co-author of **The Happiness Diet**. An anxiety attack may be an indicator of low blood sugars and the best thing one can do is to eat something that is quick yet sustaining, for example, walnuts, dark chocolate coupled with some hot tea or water.

That is for a short-term remedy however going forward, diet is very important is reducing anxiety. Consume plant-based diets, carefully picked meats and seafood, whole foods, plus lots of leafy foods, so that you can get folate and plenty of phytonutrients, which help in reducing anxiety.

Take breakfast

Dr. Ramsey also advises people not to starve themselves because most anxiety disorders are prevalent among people who skip breakfast. You could have things such as eggs, which are satisfying and filling proteins. Eggs are also loaded with choline which when in low levels lead to a rise in anxiety.

Grab foods rich in Omega 3

Although omega 3 has already been hinted on when talking about balanced diets, its importance cannot be stressed enough. While many of us know that fish oils help one to have a healthy heart and shield against depression, it also help in dealing with anxiety. A study done on students revealed that those that consumed 2.5 mgs of mixed omega 3 fatty acids daily for a period of 12 weeks experienced less anxiety before taking an exam compared to those that took placebo.

Experts have always recommended the consumption of foods rich in omega 3 and these foods include fishes from cold waters such as salmon, oily. For example, from 6 ounces of grilled wild salmon, you will get 3.75 g of omega 3 fatty acids. Other foods to get these fatty acids from are mussels, sardines, and anchovies.

Learn how to breathe

Breathing is a vital tool in preventing panic attacks and it also acts as a marker of how high or how low your anxiety levels for the day have been.

When breaths are shallow and short, it shows that there is stress and anxiety in one's body and brain. However, when one chooses to breath consciously while strengthening and lengthening the breath, it sends a signal to the brain that all is well and the person is relaxed.

Breathe and question

Now that you have learned how to breathe, you could add a little something to it; asking yourself silent questions. You need to stay mindful then starting the questioning process. These questions need to be kept simple. You could ask you something like, 'what is the temperature of the air entering my nostrils?', 'How does the air feel as it gets into my lungs?' Remember to sit comfortably, close your eyes then focus on how your breath is getting in and out of your nostrils.

Learning how to breathe will help you not to hyperventilate when experiencing a panic attack or anxiety because you will be able to remain calm.

Create a vision board

Does the future look big and scary? Then it is time for you to change your thoughts about what lies ahead. Sometimes something as small as setting permanent goals can help to take the edge off of anxiety. You could take sometime and come up with a vision board that puts excitement and thrill in the possibilities and projects that lie ahead. If you are not crafty, you could create that board online using Pininterest for that much needed inspiration. During the process of making this board, put some questions your way like; is my thought truthful, inspiring, needed and kind? This is what I call the T.H.I.N.K tool. If your answer is no, then let go of the thought and focus on another thought.

Get playful a bit

Children and animals seem to have that ability within them of playing without caring about what the next meal will consist of or if their bed is made. Most companies and organizations organize things such as team building but these happen once in 30 days. So what will you do in the other 29 days to deal with anxiety and stress? That is why you need to be responsible enough to create your own playtime. You could ask your neighbor if it is okay to walk their dog for them or ask a friend if you could babysit for them for the afternoon. This will give your mind a chance to conjure up ideas that do not bring stress and anxiety your way.

Be quiet for some time

It will not present itself to you, so you have to plan it; a time when you totally let go. Make it a point to begin with a period of time you can sustain and work with, even 5 minutes will do. This time means that the TV is off, phones are switched off and there is nothing to disturb your peace and quiet. However, before you do that, you need to let people know that you will be out of reach. This is so you avoid a scenario where once you get out of your 'silent time' you are bombarded with calls from people asking you why your phone was off, telling you how you missed an appointment and then the anxiety levels just shoot up again.

Being silent for a while is great because studies have shown that a lot of noise can enhance high stress levels. So schedule this time together with all you have to do for the day.

Conclusion

Thank you for making it through to the end of Meditation Techniques: 21 Steps That Will Lead You to Happiness. Let's hope it was informative and able to provide you with all of the tools you need to achieve your goals—whatever they may be. The topic of meditation and its beneficial effects is huge and can hardly be captured in a single book. Meditation is a life-long journey, filled with wonders and benefits. It can improve your health, teach you to be happier in your everyday life, and perhaps even offer a path to achieve inner peace most people can only dream of.

The next step is to continue practicing your meditation—regularly and with sincere intent. You can include as little or as much of the spiritual teachings meditation offers into your life. Either way, practical meditation using the techniques outlined in this short book will make a positive difference in your life—as long as you choose to meditate. The claims for the benefits of taking a spiritual approach to meditation may seem extreme, yet meditation has been tested and improved upon for thousands of years. Who can say what rewards await those who follow its path?

www.ingramcontent.com/pod-product-compliance
Lightning Source LLC
Chambersburg PA
CBHW072006070526
44583CB00015B/1355